JAPAN TRAVEL GUIDE

Your Ultimate Travel Guide for Unforgettable Journeys, Must-Do's, and Local Secrets with 100 Tips & Expert Hacks

FRED HUM

CONTENTS

Introduction

Are you intrigued by the idea of embarking on a journey to explore the world? Isn't the longing to travel driven by a sense of curiosity about the diverse possibilities that the world holds? Traveling transcends mere geographical movement; it represents a profound journey of discovery, an exploration of new perspectives, and an opportunity to immerse oneself in the richness of different cultures. When you travel, you place yourself in a unique position to learn from scratch about others and their ways of life. Each destination boasts its own distinctiveness and specialties, inviting you to embrace adventure, step out of your comfort zone, and see life through a new lens. Furthermore, travel offers you the chance to connect with individuals from diverse backgrounds, fostering understanding and cultivating empathy. Japan, a country widely recognized for its enchanting cherry blossoms, captivating anime, and delectable sushi, is a multifaceted tapestry of cultural wonders and natural beauty. However, Japan's allure extends far beyond these well-known attractions, offering a wealth of experiences waiting to be explored. This travel guide is your gateway to a transformative journey through this captivating nation. Through this comprehensive guide, we aim to immerse you in the heart of Japan, delving into its rich history, diverse landscapes, vibrant culture, and captivating attractions. Our goal is to provide you with an in-depth understanding of Japan's myriad offerings, empowering you to curate an unforgettable itinerary tailored to your interests and preferences. We understand that the process of making travel decisions can be overwhelming. This book is tailored to alleviate any doubts or concerns you may have about embarking on a journey to Japan. By offering profound insights into the mystique and allure of Japan, our guide aims to equip you with the knowledge and confidence to make informed choices and plan a remarkable travel experience

Japan: Land of the Rising Sun

Japan, a fascinating island nation situated in East Asia, is made up of a collection of islands nestled in the vast Pacific Ocean. Its archipelago spans about 1500 miles from the northeast to the southwest.

The four primary islands that constitute Japan are Hokkaido, Honshu, Shikoku, and Kyushu, with the largest island being Honshu. Additionally, Japan boasts numerous

smaller islands, including the Ryukyu Islands, as well as the Izu, Bonin, and Volcano Islands.

Tokyo, the capital, is located on the island of Honshu (*Japan | History, Flag, Map, Population, & Facts*, 2024).

This book will begin tracing the roots of Japan's history, from ancient times to the modern era. It will highlight key events, figures, and cultural developments that have shaped the nation into what it is today.

It will further transition into the exploration of Japan's scenic landscapes, from the serene beauty of its countryside, to the bustling lives of its urban settlers. Whether you want to see the cherry blossom-lined trees of Kyoto, or hike through the scenic Japanese Alps, you'll be fascinated.

You'll also come across the sandy white beaches of Okinawa. Without a doubt, Japan's natural beauty will leave you awestruck.

Next, you'll be introduced to the dazzling yet rich culture of Japan from ancient traditions such as ceremonies and kabuki theaters, to the rise of modern pop culture phenomena such as anime and manga.

Your taste buds will also be satisfied along the way, fret not. Simply reading about Japan's cuisine is bound to leave you wanting for more. The food is known for its meticulous preparation and fresh ingredients.

From foods such as sushi to ramen and tempura, you can expect loads of diversity in your eatery options.

Furthermore, you'll also get the golden chance to explore Japan's rich history by visiting centuries old castles, shrines, and temples all scattered throughout the country. Areas such as the iconic Himeji castle, and enthralling Kinkaku-ji of Kyoto.

You'll get to experience all of this, just through the ink on papers. We'll also enlighten you about omotenashi, the Japanese spirit of hospitality through various anecdotes and real experiences.

Himeji castle   Kinkaku-ji of Kyoto

Japan is an enchanting destination, offering something for every type of traveler. From the attractions to the culture, you'll for sure find something of your liking. This is what makes Japan the ideal pick.

Important Factors to Consider When Traveling to Japan

Obviously, you can't just up and leave for Japan or any country for that matter. It is imperative that you consider some factors beforehand.

- Ensure that your visa has validity, and check the visa requirements for your nationality.

- Japan undergoes many distinct seasons, and each of them offer a unique experience. Consider the weather patterns and seasonal attractions. Remember to pack your clothes according to that as well.

- Research transport options. Japan has an extensive and efficient transport network system throughout the country. You can also book a Japan Rail Pass for your feasibility (*Japan Rail Pass (JR Pass) - Trains*, 2023).

- You can choose accommodations according to your liking as well. The country offers wide range options such as traditional ryokans, modern hotels, guesthouses, and capsule hotels.

- Although most of the major tourist spots support the English language and signage, it is still better to learn a few, basic phrases. This will help alleviate your overall experience.

- Be mindful of the local rules and regulations. Even though Japan is relatively a safe country, it is better to familiarize yourself with the healthcare options. Don't carry any unnecessary or expensive items that may attract unwanted attention.

Adhere to these rules, and the ones that will be explained further in the book, and you're good to go. Maintaining an overall element of respect for the country's heritage will make your visit even smoother.

What Can You Expect From This Book?

By the time you finish reading this book, you will have gained an in-depth understanding of Japan's multifaceted identity. This comprehensive guide promises to offer you not only valuable insights but also a great deal of inspiration. Throughout the pages, you will embark on a journey through Japan's rich history, immersing yourself in its vibrant culture, admiring its diverse landscapes, and discovering a multitude of attractions. As a reader, this book is designed to transport you to Japan through vivid descriptions and provide you with practical travel advice. The expertly curated content aims to equip you with a wealth of quality knowledge and information. Let this expert handbook be your indispensable companion as you explore the treasures, uncover the secrets,

Let's Begin!

Please allow me to reassure you that our Japan Travel Guide is unlike any other travel guide you've ever seen. It's a comprehensive journey through the vibrant country, packed with essential facts. You'll be able to experience the splendor of Japan through its pages, enhance your understanding, and gain knowledge about the country's stunning landscapes, culture, and allure. It will leave you feeling inspired to explore its wonders in greater depth. So, without further ado, let's get started with the first chapter, which will provide you with an introduction to all there is to know about Japan.

CHAPTER 1

Introduction to Japan

Konnichiwa to Japan, a land of captivating contrasts! Japan, an often overlooked island nation, is a breathtaking blend of pristine natural landscapes, intricate history, cuttingedge technology, and a rich tapestry of cultural traditions. This enchanting country expertly balances the emotive allure of its time-honored beauty with the awe-inspiring architecture of its modernity. Prepare to have your expectations not only met but surpassed, as you immerse yourself in the wealth of history and culture that Japan has to offer. The gentle elegance of cherry blossoms, coupled with the pervasive sense of serenity and reverence that infuses every aspect of Japanese society, promises to exceed your anticipated experience and leave you in awe

Land of the Rising Sun

Japan is commonly known as the land of the Rising Sun. However, that is not the only name it has been given. According to the ancient Japanese tradition, the archipelago received various poetic nicknames, especially regarding its natural landscape.

Toyo ashihara no mizuho no kuni (the fertile land where reeds grow in abundance by the water's edge and where rice and the four other bowls of cereals ripen), *Yamato* (the entrance to the mountain), and *Toyo-ashihara chiiho-aki no mizuho no kuni* (the land of rich ears of the 1,500 autumns, of the plains of abundant reeds) are all titles that Japan has been known for (S.V., 2020). However, the one nickname that has stuck through time is 'land of the rising sun 'and there are various historical, geopolitical, cultural, and religious reasons for it.

The creation of this title can be traced back to the 7th century. At this time, the Chinese Empire was actively tainting the image and name of Japan by using unflattering nicknames for it. One such title was *Wa* which translates to 'dwarf 'or 'submissive, 'a jab at both the Japanese and their country.

In response, the Japanese elite began devising their own titles for the country which is when the association with the sun first emerged. *Hi no moto* (country of the origin of the sun) and *Hi-takami no kuni* (the country where the sun is seen high) were among the initial nicknames until Prince Shotoku (574-622) in 608 wrote a letter addressing the Chinese Emperor Yang de Sui.

The letter was addressed as, "The Son of Heaven in the country where the sun rises addresses a letter to the Son of Heaven in the country where the sun sets" (S.V., 2020). This was the first mention of the term *Nihhon* or *Nippon* which translates to 'land of the rising sun. 'It has since commonly been used to refer to Japan.

Apart from this assertion of dominance over the Chinese, the title 'land of the rising sun ' also holds significance in Japanese culture and mythology. The sun is an essential symbol in the archipelago because of the *Shintoism* belief system that is rooted in the praise of Amaterasu, the sun deity. One reason for this dedication to the sun deity is that according to the Japanese ancient scriptures, all the Japanese emperors were direct descendants of Amaterasu.

Its importance can further be gleaned from the special place the sun holds in Buddhism. The Buddhist tradition is devoted to the historical Buddha who transformed into a luminous being and came to be known as Dainichi Nyorai or the Great Sun. If this does not sum up the significance of the sun for Japanese culture and people, the fact that the Japanese flag prominently displays the sun symbol should do it!

Rich Cultural Heritage

Japan's cultural heritage and the customs that have been preserved are both intriguing and humbling due to the fact that Japan is an old nation. The tradition of bowing when one is in the company of an elder person or someone whom one respects is still practiced today. A gesture of reverence for one's god, the old ritual may be traced back to ancient times. It was expected that the width of the bow would increase in proportion to the rank of the individual. The practice of tattooing, the practice of shamans, and the practice of fortune telling are all essential components of the distinctive Japanese culture. Other traditions that are extensively performed in the nation include hanami, which is the practice of admiring the unrivaled beauty of blossoms, onsen, which are baths in hot springs, and performing arts. The Japanese honor these traditions by holding a number of festivals that are both bright and warm on a yearly basis. The celebrations of these events entail re-creating historical cultural practices via the mediums of theater and dance, as well as appreciating the splendor of nature. There are several aesthetic historical sites in Japan that have been meticulously conserved, and these sites are another source of Japan's rich culture. Examples of these cultural treasures are the Horiyuji Temple, which is the oldest wooden construction that has survived to this day, and the Hiroshima Geenbaku Dome, which is the only structure that has survived that existed prior to the atomic bombing. In addition, the Himeji Castle is the example of a Japanese feudal castle that has been kept in the most exquisite preservation. Each and every one of these structures and locations proudly embrace and exhibit Japan's extensive cultural past as a badge of honor

Horiyuji Temple   Hiroshima Geenbaku Dome

The Himeji Castle

Geographical Diversity

Japan not only boasts a rich culture and tradition but an equally mind-blowing blend of geographical diversity.

The archipelago comprises four breathtaking islands (Kyushu, Honshu, Shikoku, and Hokkaido) with several other smaller islands. Embracing these islands is a rich geography of mountains, water bodies, coastlines, plains, and the beautiful four seasons you can enjoy throughout the year.

75% of the land area in Japan comprises mountains (studyinjpn, 2023). Notable mountain ranges include the Japanese Alps and Mount Fuji which is the highest peak in Japan at 3,776 meters (collegesidekick, 2023). Interestingly, Japan is also home to an active volcano.

A serene contrast to the mountainous beauty of Japan is its coastal areas. The Pacific Ocean bordering the country from the east and the Japan Sea meeting it at the west ensures many coastlines and a healthy maritime culture.

Complimenting this dream-like geographical landscape are the beautiful seasons that embrace the land with a unique zeal. The heartily blooming cherry blossoms in the spring and the warm spectrum of colors in the autumn dreamily paint the country.

Key Takeaways

- Japan's identity as the 'land of the rising sun 'is rooted in historic geopolitical conflicts, its rich culture of mythology, and its devoted sense of religion.

- The archipelago is home to many unique traditions. These range from the celebration of nature and culture through theaters and festivals to cultural practices of fortune telling, shaman, and bowing.

- The diversity of Japan's cultural heritage is unmissable with many sites linking to historic, cultural, or religious events.

- Japan enjoys a natural win with its diverse landscape and the seasonal variety that it experiences.

CHAPTER 2

Planning Your Japanese Trip

Embarking on a journey to Japan is equivalent to stepping into a realm where tradition meets modernity. It's a place where beautiful landscapes co-exist with the busy metropolises. Where culinary delights of many variations are bound to tantalize the taste buds.

However, before you dive head first into this adventure, one must know that meticulous planning is essential. It's important to ensure you have an unforgettable adventure. One that you would always want to recount.

Whether you are a first time visitor, or a seasoned traveler, Japan offers an experience that lingers in your soul long after departure.

In this chapter, we'll cover all the topics that would aid you in planning a seamless Japanese trip!

Ideal Seasons to Visit

Japan is a country you would enjoy visiting any time of the year. Each season has its own highlights, and can fit to be your ideal pick.

Although it majorly depends on what type of trip you want to make, spring and autumn tend to be the most scenic times to witness Japan's beauty (Port, 2023).

Spring (March to May)

Spring is arguably the most popular time to visit Japan, thanks to the enchanting and mesmerizing cherry blossom (sakura) trees. This season, from early March to May, is the peak travel time.

Tourists and locals flock to areas such as parks, gardens and trees. This is where the country bursts into a sea of pink and white.

During this time the temperatures are mild, making it the perfect time to explore without the scorching heat or bitter cold.

Summer (June to September)

Summers in Japan are hot and humid. Temperatures range from 21 to 32 degrees celcius. (69.8 - 89.6 degrees Fahrenheit) July and August are commonly the most humid times of the entire year.

Summer is one of the most liveliest times to be in Japan.

While it can be harder to explore urban areas such as Tokyo, it's the perfect time to explore Japan's northern regions like Hokkaido, where the weather is cooler.

Summers can be exciting because of the festivals and fireworks (hanabi) that dazzle on display. From Kyoto's Gion Matsuri to Osaka's Tenjin Matsuri, and Tokushima's Awa Odori. Whether you're in Tokyo for the famous Sumida River Fireworks or exploring smaller towns, you're guaranteed a breathtaking show!

A great way to enjoy the 300-year-old Sumidagawa Fireworks Festival in Tokyo is by taking a yakatabune (riverboat) tour. Though it might cost a bit more, it's well worth it to escape the huge crowds, which can reach up to one million people (McElhinney, n.d.).

Fall (Mid September to Early December)

After spring, fall is known as the best time to visit. Depending on the location, the temperatures can vary from 10 to 21 degree celcius (50 - 69.8 degrees Fahrenheit).

Fall is renowned for its breathtaking foliage, known as koyo. This is when the country's landscapes turn into an enthralling decoration of red, orange, and gold. Jazz music fills the streets of Sendai City and lures devoted fans during the Jōzenji Street Jazz Festival.

One of the famous festivals during this time has to be the Nihonmatsu Lantern Festival in Fukushima. This is where the streets are aglow with thousands of colorful lanterns (guide, 2023).

What makes this festival stand out is the amazing artistry behind every lantern. They adorn them with different themes and pictures, showing stories from both the past and the present.

Winter (December to February)

Like many countries throughout the globe, Japan also receives fewer tourists during this time. This is mostly because people tend to visit more during the spring and fall times.

Winters are extremely cold in Japan, ranging in temperatures from 7 to -1 degree celcius. (44.6 - 30.2 degrees Fahrenheit). This makes it the perfect time to enjoy the Japanese hot springs.

In places such as Hokkaido and the Japanese Alps, you can enjoy fantastic skiing and snowboarding. Some of the cities are transformed with beautiful light displays and offer mouthwatering seasonal dishes like hot pot (nabe) and piping hot bowls of ramen during the winter. While it can get chilly, Japan's winter is generally milder compared to other destinations.

Visa and Entry Information

Some of the countries have visa exemption agreements with Japan, allowing travelers to enter for tourism or short-term stays without a visa (*So You've Landed In Japan – Arrival Procedures*, 2020).

For a hassle-free arrival, apply for your visa early. Remember to book flights in advance for the best deals, and ensure your visa remains valid six months past your stay. You can use the Henley Passport Index to see if you require a visa to enter Japan

Once you land, follow airport signage for immigration and customs procedures, ensuring your documents are ready and accessible. Cooperate with the immigration officers and keep your baggage ticket safe.

Lastly, don't hesitate to ask for assistance if you need to. It's better to ask for help, then do something that could raise suspicions.

Budgeting and Currency

When planning your Japanese trip, come up with a budget that would be flexible for your finances. Make an estimate of how much you would be spending on meals, accommodations, and activities.

Use credit cards for convenience, but keep cash handy for smaller places. It's best if you get TransferWise.

Transferwise is online banking that allows you to hold up to 40 currencies in your account. It's perfect for travelers as it allows you to make free accounts in multiple currencies (*A Simple Guide to Money When Travelling in Japan*, 2019).

With an international card there are limited places that you can get out cash. You need to find a 7-11. These are the best spots for cheap dinners, which will have ATMs that accept foreign cards.

Japan's currency is the Japanese Yen (JPY). Stay on top of expenses and exchange rates for a smooth trip.

Essential Packing List

Make a list curated for your comfort and fashion. When packing for Japan, it's necessary to have a list that meets the needs for the country's climate, and your planned activities.

Pick clothes that are versatile in their function. For Japan's varied weather, include lightweight layers for warmer days, and warmer clothing for cooler evenings. Don't forget to pack comfortable walking shoes, as exploring Japan often involves a lot of walking.

Don't forget the following items when packing as well!

- Toiletries
- Sunscreen (SPF 50 is recommended)
- Portable chargers
- Guidebook
- Medications (if any)
- Waterproof jackets
- Umbrellas

Carry your travel documents and snacks for the journey. These are a must-have if you want to ensure a comfortable yet enjoyable stay in Japan!

Key Takeaways

- Spring or fall is the best time to visit Japan.

- You won't need a visa to travel if Japan provides a visa exemption for your country.

- Use a 7-11 for affordable dinners and access to the Japanese Yen easily.

- Ensure to pack multi-functional clothes and comfortable shoes.

CHAPTER 3

Getting Around Japan

In a land where ancient traditions effortlessly blend with cutting-edge technology, embarking on a journey through Japan is a captivating adventure that promises both enchantment and efficiency.

Amidst the scenic landscapes and bustling energy, it's important you understand the intricate web of Japanese transportation systems. Transportation is an essential part of any traveling journey, and should highly be considered when planning to make a visit.

Whether you want to speed across the countryside aboard a bullet train, or if you want to glide in sleek subway carriages; you best believe it will require punctuality and precision.

As you embark on the journey through the Land of the Rising Sun, let its rhythm of transportation network be your trusted guide.

From the swift trains to the quaint rickshaws, each mode of transport in Japan offers a distinct view of this captivating country. Get ready for an unforgettable journey that will leave a lasting impression on your soul.

Now that you have finally made it to Japan, let's discover how you'll be traveling to your favorite spots around the country!

Rail and Bus Network

One of the most famous ways of traveling to Japan has to be on Shinkansen bullet trains!

If you don't know, Shinkansen bullet trains are the fastest and convenient way to discover all that Japan has in store for its avid travelers.

The extensive Japan Rail (JR) network, has bullet trains zipping at a top speed of 320 km/h (199 mph), ensuring swift travel to any destination (*Shinkansen: Bullet Trains in Japan | JRailPass*, n.d.).

There are a total of nine Shinkansen lines that stretch across all over Japan. Starting from Tokyo and heading south is the Tokaido Shinkansen, linking the capital to Osaka. From Osaka, the Sanyo Shinkansen continues to Fukuoka, where the Kyushu Shinkansen then traverses Kyushu island from north to south.

Other lines radiate northward or inland from Tokyo. These include the Akita, Hokkaido, Hokuriku, Joetsu, Tohoku, and Yamagata Shinkansen lines. The Hokkaido line extends furthest north, all the way to Hokkaido island.

You must keep this in mind that while traveling Japan, you will want to have affordable options as your first priority.

The Japan Rail Pass is an exclusive deal for foreigners visiting on a temporary basis. It allows you to take as many rides as you want throughout the country (*Japan Rail Pass | Guide | Travel Japan*, n.d.).

Let's explore some of the common options available for an easy and satisfying trip!

Subways

In cities like Tokyo and Osaka, the subway options are easier to use as they connect key attractions and neighborhoods. Frequent services and an increase of English signage, makes the exploring of these cities simple and favorable.

For a day of exploration within Tokyo, consider opting for a Tokyo Subway Pass (Tan, 2023).

The pass offers you the flexibility to choose from passes valid for 24, 48, or 72 hours, making it tailored to your schedule.

Local Trains

Local trains and subways work hand in hand with each other. There are several types of local trains that differ by how many stops they make.

These local trains provide access to suburban areas and neighboring towns nearby. If you want to venture to the enchanting spots on the outskirts of Kyoto or explore traditional villages near Hiroshima, local trains offer a convenient mode of transport.

However, the most iconic travel hack for touring Japan has to be the IC card.

Just like London's Oyster card, Hong Kong's Octopus card, and New York City's MetroCard, Japan's IC cards are your ticket to easy city exploration (*Train Travel in Japan: A Comprehensive Guide*, n.d.).

Not only does this rechargeable card cover your public transportation fares, but also lets you buy items at convenience stores and vending machines.

That sure does sound like a win-win situation!

Buses

Buses also play a vital role in urban transportation, particularly for reaching destinations not served by trains or subways.

They are the second most popular option in Japan after trains (Brown, 2023). While it may seem scary at first, especially outside major cities due to limited English translations, navigating buses becomes easier with practice.

There are two main options when it comes to buses; city buses and charter buses. City buses operate within urban areas, costing under 500 yen, with boarding areas near stations.

As for the charter buses, unlike city buses, they have fixed fares instead of distance-based pricing.

In addition, for added comfort, many buses also accept payment via IC cards!

Diverse Transportation Options

Beyond the mentioned options, there are various other transportation methods available to explore Japan's diverse landscapes and vibrant cities.

For example, you can opt for a rental service for your touring spots. Japan offers rental cars for scenic road trips, providing travelers with the freedom to explore the country's beautiful landscapes and attractions at their own pace.

Explore options such as taxis and ride-sharing options. Don't want to go with any of those? Opt for a bicycle! The cool breeze, and mind-blowing sights are going to enhance your visit even more!

Taking a road trip to visit scattered areas in the country isn't the only way. You can choose domestic flights for island-hopping and long-distance travel as well.

Practical Tips and Resources

Traveling to Japan is an exciting feeling in itself. However, it can be stressful planning your navigation and routes.

Here are some of the best tools or options for ensuring seamless journeys throughout Japan:

- Google Maps.

- Japan Travel by NAVITIME (van Hout, 2023).

- GuruNavi (finding the best restaurants in Japan)

- Japan Official Travel App.

- VoiceTra (speech translation app)

With the help of such options to get around Japan, it's safe to say that you will be in good hands.

These apps and sources will aid in planning your trip efficiently. They will be helping you in avoiding incidents such as getting lost, or offending any local because of misheard utterance or wrong interpretation of the language.

In addition to that, while you're traveling to one of the most beautiful destinations in the world, don't forget to capture your memories.

Also, craft unforgettable experiences by exploring scenic train routes all across Japan!

Key Takeaways

- Understand that it's important to plan your transport options just as much as the rest of the trip.

- One can opt for bullet/local trains, rent car services, buses, subways, and many more options.

- Get the Japan Rail Pass for unlimited passes to move around.

- Download travel apps to ensure smoother organization of your most awaited trip.

CHAPTER 4

Tokyo Unveiled

A city that is so large that even the locals may not be able to fully appreciate or comprehend it in their lifetime. Let's walk through the wonders and life of Tokyo, the largest city and metropolitan area in the world!

The city of Tokyo is a fascinating blend of the traditional and contemporary. The harmony of tradition, technology, culture, and innovation found in this city keeps you coming back for more. Tokyo is an exciting destination not just for first-time explorers but also for those who've experienced its thrill before. You just can't have enough!

As we begin to unravel this mysterious metropolis you should know that Tokyo is at the heart of Japan. It is found in the southern Kanto region, located at the approximate center of the country.

This geographical location is what gives Tokyo a rich natural diversity. Tokyo is bordered by the Edogawa River and the Chiba prefecture on the east, the Yamanashi prefecture and magnificent mountains on the west, the Tamagawa River on the south, and the Saitama prefecture on the north.

Tokyo's diversity is most notable across its 23 special wards into which the city is divided. Each of these districts and neighborhoods has its own distinct personality, vibe, and charm! From traditional and cultural centers to fashion hubs and anime towns, you'll find something unique in each of these neighborhoods.

Tokyo is disclosed as an energetic city with various events and interesting things to do.

Here are some fun things to do in Tokyo:

Unique Attractions

TeamLab Borderless:

An exhibit facility in Odaiba that hosts digital art and which provides an extraordinary feeling with installations that can be touched.

Ghibli Museum:

This museum is entirely themed after Studio Ghibli and offers a variety of things about My Neighbor Totoro, Spirited Away and more.

Odaiba:

This island of the future has shopping centers, cinemas and attractions such as Gundam statue and Joypolis.

Amusement Parks and Arcades

Tokyo Disneyland and Disney Sea: Tokyo Disneyland Theme park first opened to the public in 1983. It has broad areas of interest with attractions such as Cinderella's Castle, Space Mountain and Pirates of Caribbean, its areas include Adventureland, Fantasyland, and Tomorrowland. It has an amazingly exotic flavour of Japanese style mixed together with the traditional Disney fairy-tale charm. There are parades, live performances, and the holiday events, ensuring that children of all ages have a wonderful time.

Odaiba Joypolis: An arcade that can be likened to an indoor fun fairs that consist of fun games, roller coasters and games that simulates virtual reality.

Akihabara: is a vibrant Tokyo neighborhood and the hub of anime lovers in east Tokyo! The exciting array of maid cafes, arcades, and many anime and comic stores is why anime enthusiasts flock to this place. You'll find neon lights, a spirited vibe, and lively colors, and the biggest anime and comic stores!

Food Adventures

Street Food: Savor eats from food carts including takoyaki (octopus balls), taiyaki (fish-shaped cakes), and yakitori (grilled skewered chicken/pork).

Themed Cafes: Go to quirky animal cafes such as the Owl Cafe, Hedgehog Café Harry, Mame Shiba Café, Café Hoshinoko, Sakuragaoka goat cafe and Dog Heart to name a few. There are also options for general themed cafes; Robot Restaurant, Pokémon Cafe, Harry Potter Café, Reissue Cafe.

Ramen Shops: Explore various ramens from some of the famous restaurants such as, Ichiran, Ippudo, and Tsuta which was recognized as the first Michelin starred ramen restaurant.

Parks and Recreation

1. **Yoyogi Park:** Great for picnicking, viewing pedestrians and other performances especially of the art variety on the weekends.

Shinjuku Gyoen National Garden

Ueno Zoo: The oldest in Japan that can be found in Ueno Park and that houses giant pandas among others.

Sumida Aquarium: This is a new aquarium that is situated at Tokyo Skytree Town It has amazingly designed tanks and has quite different marine life.

Shopping

Takeshita Street: A popular pedestrian and shopping area in the mixed Harajyu district with loads of shops, cafes, and trendy designer clothes stores.

Don Quijote: A well-known store that will sell almost everything from chips to computers, is available for buyers 24/7.

Tsukiji Outer Market: As for the inner market, it has shifted and evolved through the years while the outer market is still a great place to find food and particularly seafood.

Cultural Experiences

Sumo Wrestling: Go to a sumo bout or watch them practice in the morning. The main sumo arena, the Ryogoku Kokugikan, is where visitors to Tokyo may experience sumo wrestling. In the Ryogoku neighborhood, this is a well-known arena that hosts three of the six Grand Sumo Tournaments, which take place in January, May, and September. In addition to attending during the competitions, fans may learn more about the sport by going to the Sumo Museum housed inside the Kokugikan. Additionally, visitors may see the morning training sessions of the sumo wrestlers in stable houses like Arashio Beya. A detailed peek into the world of sumo, which combines sport and culture, is provided by all of these encounters

Kabuki Theater: Visit the Kabuki-za Theatre in Ginza to watch the conventional Japanese theatre, called Kabuki.

Tea Ceremony: Visit temples and gardens like Happo-en or go to a regular tea ceremony in a proper tea house.

That's why everyone who is in Tokyo will surely find something exciting to do there as the city has something for everyone. There is always something to do in this evolving city; be it culture, technology, food or even out-of-the-ordinary experiences.

Sightseeing and Landmarks

Tokyo Tower and Tokyo Skytree: Skyscrapers which provide some breathtaking views of the City. Tokyo Tower is an elegant historic landmark modeled after the Eiffel Tower in Paris in 1958.

Senso-ji Temple: The temple that was originally constructed at the heart of Tokyo in Asakusa.

Meiji Shrine: A scenic Shinto shrine located in the heart of the city opened in the middle to the forest in Shibuya.

Imperial Palace: Originally a royal place, impressing the visitor to the Emperor of Japan and his family, included splendid gardens accessible to the public.

Neighborhoods to Explore

Shibuya: For the primary landmarks like Shibuya Crossing and the neon nightlife.

Harajuku: is the chic fashionista district of Tokyo. Here you'll find people following the latest trends and wearing the latest fashion. Takeshita Street is packed with wonderfully eccentric fashion stores to shop your heart out

Ginza: A center with expensive stores and shops; with apparel stores being exclusive and commercial stores being departmental.

Asakusa: is known as the historical and cultural district of Tokyo. The neighborhood has a cozy old-town vibe with little streets, traditional temples and architecture, and stalls on nearby streets that appear to have been preserved since ancient times. There's always some festival going on in this neighborhood and if you visit it in April, you can experience Hanami, the sakura blossom viewing festival!

Roppongi: is the perfect contrast to the old-town vibe of Asakusa. It is known as the nightlife center of Tokyo. Roppongi is like a city within a city with its modern and massive developments and the streets hustling and bustling with busy office workers by the day and people out to drink and party at night! Here's where you'll find some of the most classy restaurants and the best gourmet in Tokyo.

Museums and Culture

Tokyo National Museum: A part of the Ueno Park and is the largest museum in Japan.

Mori Art Museum: Modern art museum with art pieces that include Japanese and foreign artists.

Ghibli Museum: A definite have to see for people who enjoy watching animation Studio Ghibli has to offer.

Parks and Nature

Ueno Park: It is large park that also houses museums, a zoo, ferris wheel and in spring, cherry blossom trees.

Yoyogi Park: A great park in Tokyo that can be effectively used for outdoor concerts, picnics, and sports and has many people passing by near Meiji Shrine.

Shinjuku Gyoen National Garden: in Shibuyu is a renowned location for Hanami during spring. It's home to a breathtaking plantation of cherry blossom trees.

Rikugien Garden: A small but pleasant chasz with traditional elements referring to Japanese gardens, especially in the autumn and spring.

Shopping and Entertainment

Akihabara: It is famously known as the land of the electronics, anime and Manga.

Odaiba: A commercial and entertainment hub along with an art attraction, the teamLab Borderless museum.

Tsukiji Outer Market: A very good establishment for delicious and all-fresh fish and seafood.

① Akihabara

② Asakusa

③ Roppongi

④ Yoyogi Park

⑤ Shinjuku Gyoen National Garden

⑥ Tokyo Tower

⑦ Harajuku

Culinary Delights

From fresh and fast-selling seafood and traditional Japanese snacks to fine restaurants with world-class cuisine, Tokyo has got it all!

The Tsukiji Outer Market is a world-famous spot for food enthusiasts and tourists! The market is a treasure trove with fresh ingredients, seafood, spices, traditional sweets, and everything you need to produce exotic food.

The Tokyo food scene is incomplete without fresh seafood! From sushi to tempura, all kinds of fish and seafood dishes are produced using traditional recipes and successful innovation.

The food scene in Tokyo is part of the larger cultural experience with the traditional tea ceremonies and sake which has historically been drunk in religious and cultural ceremonies and social gatherings.

Apart from the local and traditional food, Tokyo flaunts many Michelin-starred and high- end restaurants with a fine dining experience. Whether you prefer an upscale food experience and thrive on sampling the local street food, the innovative food scene in Tokyo will surprise you!

Dishes that you must try include

- **Sushi** at Sushi no Midori or at Mantenzushi. They're both popular sushi restaurants in Tokyo offering amazing sushi dishes!

- **Yakitori**, or grilled chicken skewers is a traditional Japanese dish cooked over charcoal grills. You must try both salt only and tare sauce seasonings with it!

- **Ramen** is an authentic noodle experience that you must have in Tokyo! This centuries-old dish and a staple is served in a flavorful broth with various ingredients such as green onions, sliced pork, seaweed, bamboo shoots, etc.

- **Okonomiyaki** are Japanese savory pancakes. You'll find these in many renowned restaurants in Tokyo in a variety such as Negiyaki Okonomiyaki, Hiroshimayaki Okonomiyaki, and Monjayaki Okonomiyaki.

Key Takeaways

- Tokyo's vastness cannot be comprehended in a single lifetime.

- Tokyo is a seamless blend of traditional and contemporary times, vents, and festivals.

- The diverse neighborhoods of Tokyo each hold a unique, exotic, and wonderful charm and have plenty of authentic Japanese experiences to offer.

- The culinary experience in Tokyo is wide-ranging from high-end restaurants to local seafood and traditional food ceremonies.

- Tokyo also captures the cultural elements with many festivals, events, and activities to immerse you in the beautiful culture of Japan.

CHAPTER 5

Kyoto's Timeless Charm

Kyoto is home to Japan's cultural and traditional aspects. Its timeless charm and serenity emerge from the treasure trove of sacred cultural properties, divine shrines, and ancient temples found in the city.

The city breathes and lives in a tranquil balance of the past and the present, housing 20% of Japan's national treasures, 14% of significant cultural assets, and 17 places that are deemed UNESCO World Heritage Sites (Kyoto Travel, 2024).

Temples and Shrines

The incredible shrines and temples of Kyoto lend it a sacred aesthetic beauty. You'll find thousands of magnificent shrines and temples of all sizes and designs across the city.

While some of these holy sites are dedicated to Buddhism, other shrines and temples ascribe to the ancient Shinto religion. This historic landscape is complemented by Kyoto's scenic beauty and the pristine air of green forests and bamboo groves populating the city.

Kiyomizu Temple

Located in the naturistic wooded hills on the east side of Kyoto is the Kiyomizu-Dera or the 'Pure Water 'temple. Visiting Kiyomizu is like traveling back in time with its ancient architecture and historic appeal. The temple is popular for its 13-meter-high wooden platform that extends from the main hall.

Many tourists flock to this temple to witness the mesmerizing view of the vibrant cherry blossoms, maple trees, and the panoramic sight of Kyoto city's center from the platform. Kiyomizu is also a highly celebrated UNESCO Heritage Site.

Kinkakuji Temple

Kinkakuji literally refers to the 'Temple of the Golden Pavilion' and is also famously known as Rokuonji or the Deer Garden Temple. This breathtaking Zen Buddhist shrine is another UNESCO Heritage Site in Kyoto.

The shrine stands 12.8 meters high with 3 floors, two of which are gorgeously decorated with gold leaf on a Japanese lacquer. A stunning Japanese-style garden surrounds the unique architecture of the shrine that will bless your eyes! You can enjoy one of the most revered traditions of tea ceremony in this shrine's traditional tea room!

Fushimi Inari Shrine

Built-in 711, Fushimi Inari is a spectacular shrine characterized by its many vibrant orange torii gates. The beautiful gates lead up to the mountain known as Mount Inari. The shrine is dedicated to the fox, known as inari, as it is believed to protect the annual harvest.

You need to hike for about 2 hours to reach the summit of Mount Inari. However, for a more convenient route, you can take the Keihan line at the Fushimi Inari station.

Yasaka Shrine

Also known as the Gin Shrine, the Yasaka shrine is a beautiful remnant of the grand temple that once stood. Constructed in the 7th century, this shrine is a significant center of the Gion festival.

The shrine is dedicated to the deity Susanoo-no-Mikoto who is a symbol of prosperity and protection from pestilence. There is a beautiful ritual you can partake in when you visit the shrine. It involves writing your wishes, thoughts, or prayers on a small piece of paper and tying it to the tree covered with many paper bows!

1. Kiyomizu Temple
2. Kinkakuji Temple
3. Fushimi Inari Shrine
4. Yasaka Shrine

Traditional Tea Houses

Tea and tea ceremonies in Japan hold immense value and stand for harmony, tranquility, respect, and purity. The ceremonies have different names such as *Chanoyu, Chado,* and *Sado,* and are focused on the gestures and movements of the host as they prepare and serve tea allowing the guests to cherish and appreciate the bowl of tea they are served.

Kyoto is known as the spiritual capital of tea in Japan given its rich history with tea ceremonies. It's where the founder of modern tea, Sen no RIky, lived and worked which is why it is the center of the practice.

Kyoto is also popular for its production of green tea, more specifically, matcha green tea. It is home to several tea houses where tourists and guests can savor and fully understand the phenomenon of tea ceremonies. Some popular tea houses in Kyoto are:

1. **CAMELLIA** is a perfect place for enjoying a formal, authentic, and peaceful tea ceremony experience wearing a kimono

The ceremony takes place in a private, traditional, sun-bathed tea room allowing you the private space to fully immerse yourself in the process. Based on your preference, you can go for either a shared or private tea experience.

1. **SAKA MARUYAMA** is your place if you prefer the classic Japanese tea house experience. It has an old-school classic interior with paper windows and wooden or bamboo architecture.

At Saka Maruyama, you not only get to choose your tea but also the teapot! Additionally, you can experience their one-of-a-kind Fukamushicha tea which is only found at this tea house.

Tea House MOTOAN is another gem for experiencing tea ceremonies. This is especially friendly to tourists and foreigners because of its easy-to-read English menu. The large tea variety, from thin tea for new tea-drinkers to thick tea which is almost like a paste, will astonish you!

The tea house has been around since the 1600s and offers a scenic atmosphere overlooking a beautiful Japanese garden.

1. CAMELLIA
2. SAKA MARUYAMA
3. Tea House MOTOAN

Geisha Districts

Kyoto is home to a total of 5 districts or hanamachi that are collectively known as Gokagai or the 'Five Flower Towns' Each of these Geisha districts is a rich blend of history, traditions, culture, and the unparalleled beauty of Japanese aesthetics and architecture.

The five districts comprise **Gion Kobu** (First Class Gion) the largest and most prestigious Gion famous for its world-class annual dances; **Gion Higashi** (Eastern Gion) which is the smallest hanamachi and produces a single annual dance called Gion Odori (Dances of Gion); **Miyagawa Cho** which is popular for the Minamiza theater and the kabuki dance- style displayed each April; **Pontocho** with its many Ochaya sitting above water providing visitors with a mesmerizing view and its annual Komogawa Odori dances (Dances of the Kamo River); and finally, the

Kamishichiken, a small yet extremely historic hanamachi with its annual showcase of Kitano Odori (Dances of the Kitano Shrine) marking the beginning of cherry blossom season.

There are many opportunities for fun, entertainment, and life in these Kyoto districts. You can visit the following places to get a taste of the life and culture of these districts

- Wander through the historic **Shirakawa Street** in the Gion district to embrace the serene beauty of the people, architecture, tall willow trees, and traditional dining places.

- **Hanami Lane** has some of the most gorgeous historic architecture. Its charm stems from the traditional wooden townhouses known as *machiya*, art galleries, kimono stores, antique shops, etc.

- You cannot miss the **Shijo Dori,** a famous shopping street dedicated to those with fancy and high-end choices. Passing through the Gion district it strikes a stunning blend of modern and luxury-oriented department stores and the historic, elegant charm of the Gion. You'll also find many local specialty food stalls and craft stores to enjoy!

- **Teahouses,** the best places for cultural appreciation and relaxation, will find you everywhere. Don't miss out on them!

- For an old-school experience, do explore the **Shinbashi Dori,** overlooking the glittering waters of the river with traditional, generations-old, homes lining the streets lit up with warm and glowing lanterns.

Shirakawa Street   Hanami Lane

Shijo Dori   Shinbashi Dori

Key Takeaways

- Kyoto has a rich cultural and historic wealth with many of its places part of the UNESCO World Heritage Sites.

- The city basks in the glory of many magnificent shrines and temples dedicated to Shintoism and Buddhism.

- The 5 Geisha districts of Kyoto offer much in terms of cultural learning, entertainment, food experience, shopping, and a window into the classic life and traditions of Japan.

- Kyoto is extremely popular for its tea ceremonies and tea houses.

- There is no absence of scenic beauty in Kyoto with its maple trees, lush green Japanese gardens, rivers, and scenic mountain views.

1. Shirakawa Street
2. Hanami Lane
3. Shijo Dori
4. Shinbashi Dori

CHAPTER 6

Osaka: Culinary Paradise

Food is not just for mere energy purposes. We, as humans, refer to it as the heart and soul of the human body. Consequently, Japan is one of those places where food is enjoyed to its fullest.

Osaka is often referred to by nicknames such as, "Kitchen of Japan" or the "Nation's Kitchen." It indeed is a culinary paradise that attracts food lovers from around the globe (*Osaka Food Markets: Everything You Need to Know*, 2024).

There is no better place in the world to surrender your taste buds, than in the gastronomic kingdom of Japan.

Nonetheless, let's dive deep into the fascinating allures that specifically Osaka provides its eager tourists with!

Street Food Adventures

Osaka is big on street food adventures, and this is what makes it such a dynamic place to be in the country.

The city is renowned for its bustling street food districts such as Dotonbori and Kuromon Ichiba Market, where visitors can indulge in a plethora of delicious snacks and local specialties.

Osaka is also famous for its fresh seafood, thanks to its proximity to the sea. Visitors can enjoy an array of sushi, sashimi, and seafood dishes made from the freshest ingredients available.

In addition, there is even an expression that is used for Osaka's food craze, "kuidaore," to eat oneself into financial ruin (*Osaka: A Food Paradise*, 2019).

However, let's specifically talk about Dotonbori- a renowned tourist destination. Conveniently, it is just steps away from the Namba Station, giving you the opportunity to eat till you drop, and do some shopping and sightseeing, too.

Located in the heart of Osaka, this district is unmissable. It is known for its vibrant nightlife, neon lights, and, of course, its iconic food scene. Let's look at some of the must- try local delicacies and hidden culinary gems that you shouldn't miss when visiting Dotonbori!

Takoyaki

This delicious grilled octopus dish is made of ingredients such as wheat, flour, eggs, chopped octopus, pickled ginger, and scallions. A quintessential Osaka street food, vendors often have long lines in waiting. This indicates their popularity, and fresh preparation.

It's extremely hot, as it is delicious, thus be careful when you bite into it! If you don't want to wait in lines, look for a smaller, less crowded takoyaki stand tucked away in one of the alleys.

Okonomiyaki

Next up in line is the sublime and mouth-watering okonomiyaki! Notice how this also ends with, "yaki" which means that it is something grilled!

Okonomiyaki, a savory pancake with a wheat flour base and stuffed with shredded cabbage and various proteins like squid, prawn, or octopus, as well as chicken or pork. A

drizzle of mayo, a Japanese-style Worcestershire sauce called sosu, bonito flakes, and seaweed are added to the top to finish it off.

Referred to as Japanese savory pancakes, it rose to fame during World War 2, when food was limited. Using whatever ingredients they had on hand, resulted in a flavorful and fulfilling meal born out of necessity (*Dig-In to Japan's Culinary Paradise - JAPAN AIRLINES*, n.d.).

This isn't your average pancake. In fact, okonomiyaki is something you haven't ever tried before!

Ramen

You might have had that instant ramen at home, but that's not what we are talking about here.

If you want to try the real deal, then you have to have a hearty, scrumptious, soupy bowl of ramen in Japan!

Ramen comes in three flavorful broth bases: shoyu (soy sauce), miso (soybean paste), and tonkotsu (pork).

And when you're slurping noodles in Japan or at a Japanese restaurant, embrace it! It's not only socially acceptable, but also helps cool down those yummy, flavorful noodles as you savor them.

For a tasty bowl of ramen in Osaka's Dōtonbori district, Kinryu Ramen is a must-visit (*10 Reasons Why Osaka Is a Street Food Lovers Paradise*, 2020).

However, remember that you'll find fantastic ramen all over the city, so feel free to explore other spots, too!

Explore the charming side streets branching off from the lively Dotonbori main roads to find cozy izakayas; a favorite hangout among locals.

These quaint spots offer a warm ambiance and a chance to try unique dishes while experiencing genuine Japanese dining vibes.

Historical Landmarks

Japan's Osaka Castle stands tall as a testament to the nation's storied past, offering visitors a glimpse into its feudal history.

In 1538, it was built by Hideyoshi Toyotomi. He was a powerful feudal lord and warrior during the Sengoku period. He constructed Osaka Castle amidst ongoing turmoil after years of conflict.

He was known for his obsession with gold. Thus, he adorned most of the castle's interior with it. Osaka Castle served as a stronghold under Hideyoshi's rule. It played a crucial role in ending Japan's wars and briefly uniting the nation, bringing a moment of peace (*Osaka Castle | Discover Kansai*, n.d.).

Apart from this, you can also explore other fascinating sites like the serene temples of Shitennoji and Sumiyoshi Taisha, offering glimpses into ancient traditions.

These historical gems provide a captivating backdrop to Osaka's bustling culinary scene, offering visitors a well-rounded experience of the city's cultural heritage.

1. Osaka Castle
2. Shitennoj
3. Sumiyoshi Taisha

Entertainment in Namba

Undoubtedly, Dotonbori steals the spotlight as a lively entertainment district in Namba.

Here, you'll find that the theaters offer a mix of tradition and modern performances. Shopping arcades like Shinsaibashi Shopping Arcade and Namba Walk cater to every shopper's delight.

Once the sun sets down, Dotonbori lights up with neon signs, inviting you to explore its vibrant nightlife scene filled with bars, clubs, and izakayas.

Whether you're into culture, shopping, or nightlife, Dotonbori has it all in one spectacular package!

Key Takeaways

- Osaka serves as one of the main hubs for the most delicious street foods in Japan.

- Dotonbori, located near Namba station, is the destination for treats such as grilled Japanese foods, Japanese barbeques, and authentic ramen.

- Osaka houses historical landmarks such as Osaka Castle and other shrines and temples.

- Apart from eatery stops in Namba such as Dotonbori, lively entertainment spots such as theaters, bars, clubs, can be found as well!

CHAPTER 7

Nature Retreats in Hokkaido

Japan's natural beauty is known to have a stunning blend of landscapes. The snow layered mountains, peaceful forests, and vibrant coastlines, are bound to leave you in awe! Not only are they extremely tranquil, but offer the soul a chance to retreat.

Legendary peaks such as Mount Fuji, and ancient cedar forests offer you a glimpse into Japan's rich biodiversity.

One of such spots in Japan is called Hokkaido. In this chapter, we'll be talking all there is to know, what wonders it provides, and the wildlife too.

If you are a true nature lover, Hokkaido is surely not the region to miss when traveling to Japan!

Scenic Landscapes

Hokkaido is Japan's northernmost island. It is known for its stunning natural beauty and unique cultural importance. Its vast terrain gives one the ideal mix of rugged mountains, pristine lakes, and lush forests. This makes it a paradise for outdoor enthusiasts (*Hokkaido*, n.d.).

In addition to that, Hokkaido is also known for its delectable seafood, dairy products, and winter resort spots. Let's talk about some of the majestic mountains and serene lakes!

Mount Asahidake

Better called as Hokkaido's highest peak, Mount Asahidake has breathtaking opportunities for hiking and climbing.

Serving as an active terrain, it is narrated by the Ainu people as the garden where gods play or "Kamuimintara" in the Ainu language (*Asahidake, Japan: The Mountain Where Ainu Gods Play*, 2022).

It sets an otherworldly stage for its visitors. Especially during fall when the foliage transforms into an attractive sense of colors.

Mount Rishiri

This mountain is usually identified because of its distinct cone shape. It is one of the most popular hiking spots, where you would also get to witness the lush vegetation, including forests and alpine meadows.

Mount Rishiri is nothing less than a hiker's go-to destination. It has plenty of trails, one of the most in-demand being the Rishiri Fuji Trail. This trail takes you to the top, where you'll be treated to breathtaking views of the sea and nearby islands (*Guide to Hiking Mount Rishiri (利尻山) in Japan*, n.d.).

Lake Toya

Lake Toya is a sight right out of a fairytale. It is the third-largest caldera lake hidden among the towering volcanic mountains. As a traveler or visitor, there is so much you can do. You can hop on a boat, and soak all the beauty around. If you prefer to stay on land,

you can also go for a stroll, finding solace in the picturesque environment (*8 Most Beautiful Lakes in Hokkaido*, n.d.).

There would be no better way to end the day than by visiting a hot spring resort!

Lake Onneto

Lake Onneto is a hidden gem waiting to be discovered. It is surrounded by dense forests and magical mountains (*In Japan's North, the Seasons Are Intense: 5 Gorgeous Places for Hokkaido Scenery | LIVE JAPAN Travel Guide*, 2021).

The lake enchants its visitors with its clear water and pacific atmosphere. If you want to see a sight unlike no other, make a trip in the fall. The colorful fall leaves reflect off the lake, creating a scene even more beautiful than ever.

1 Mount Asahidake
2 Mount Rishiri
3 Lake Toya
4 Lake Onneto

Winter Wonders

By the time the snowy months roll around in Hokkaido, it turns into a gigantic winter wonderland. It offers a plethora of activities and attractions to keep the travelers amused.

Snow Festivals

Hokkaido hosts some of the most famous snow festivals in Japan that people all over the world wait to visit. These snow festivals usually showcase intricate ice sculptures and dancing light displays.

One of such festivals is the annual Sapporo Snow Festival. Using a natural resource they have in abundance, a few students back in 1950 showcased some ice sculptures. Since then, it has transformed into this extravagant destination that draws millions each year.

It runs for an entire week in early February, however the preparations begin almost a month before (*Sapporo Snow Festival*, n.d.).

Ski Resorts

Hokaiddo also has some of the most classical ski resorts that catch the attention of many snow sport enthusiasts every year.

Popular Ski Resorts Niseko United

Overview:

The most well-known ski resort in Hokkaido is Niseko, which is renowned for its reliable and plentiful powder snow. It consists of Grand Hirafu, Hanazono, Niseko Village, and Annupuri, four interconnected resorts.

Tips:

- **Accommodation:** Reserve your place of stay well in advance, particularly for the busiest times of year (December to February). Budget hostels and opulent hotels are among the options.

- **Transportation**: It's simple to tour the entire area as the Niseko United Shuttle connects the four resorts. Another practical choice is to rent a vehicle.

- **Activities:** In addition to skiing, consider snowshoeing, snowmobiling, and perusing the lively après-ski scene.

Furano

Overview:

Furano provides a more laid-back skiing experience with good snow quality. It is known for its diverse terrain and less crowded than Niseko.

Tips:

- **Best Time to Visit:** When is the ideal time to visit Furano? The ideal time to ski there is usually in January and February, but the season lasts from late November to early May.

- **Lift Passes:** In order to save time and money, think about ordering lift passes online in advance.

- **Local Culture:** Experience the local flavors and customs by visiting the cheese producers and vineyards in Furano.

Rusutsu

Overview:

Rusutsu Resort is well-known for its family-friendly amenities, tree runs, and polished slopes. Three mountains are part of the resort: Mount Isola, East Mountain, and West Mountain.

Tips:

- **Family-Friendly:** There are many of kid-friendly activities available at Rusutsu, such as an indoor wave pool and an amusement park.

- **Off-Piste Skiing:** Rusutsu is well-known for its fantastic off-piste skiing possibilities. Before going off-trail, make sure to verify the laws and circumstances in your area.

- **Dining:** Take advantage of the resort's array of eating options, which include both fine dining restaurants and informal eateries.

Tomamu

Overview:

Tomamu Resort is well-known for its opulent lodgings and distinctive activities, such Japan's largest indoor wave pool, Mina-Mina Beach, and the Ice Village.

Tips:

- **Luxury Stay:** For a luxurious stay, opt for the Hoshino Resorts TOMAMU, which provide elegant accommodations and first-rate services.

- **Night Skiing:** Tomamu offers fantastic night skiing experiences that let you spend more time on the slopes.

- **Ice Village:** With its ice slides, ice bars, and exquisite ice sculptures, the Ice Village is a fantastic place to visit.

General Tips for Skiing in Hokkaido

1. **Weather and Gear:** The harsh winters and abundant snowfall of Hokkaido are well-known. Bring the appropriate equipment, such as waterproof gloves, layers of clothes, and high-quality ski goggles.

2. **Local Etiquette:** Learn about the customs and standards of Japanese skiers, like waiting your turn, steering clear of cutting in front of others, and demonstrating respect for others on the slopes.

3. **Language:** Although major resorts have a large English-speaking population, knowing a few simple Japanese phrases might be useful and appreciated by locals.

4. **Travel Insurance:** Make sure your policy covers both winter sports activities and any unforeseen medical costs.

5. **Peak Season:** Late December through February is Hokkaido's peak season. To minimize any last-minute headaches, it is highly suggested to book hotels, lift passes, and rentals in advance. Hokkaido promises a winter escape you won't soon forget, whether you're training on the slopes, admiring the glittering ice sculptures, or just want to experience the most amazing winter activities.

Wildlife Encounters

Hokkaido is also home to a variety of wildlife parks and sanctuaries that lay out the region's diverse fauna.

Shiretoko National Park

If you are a first time traveler, you are bound to ask the following question. **"What does Shiretoko mean?"**

Well, it comes from the Ainu word **"sir etok,"** which translates to **"the end of the Earth."**

Shiretoko National Park is not only one of Japan's UNESCO World Heritage Sites but also one of its most stunning national parks.

From brown bears to Steller's sea eagles, visitors can discover the rich biodiversity of Shiretoko through interactive exhibits and guided tours (*Hokkaido's Best Parks and Nature Attractions - JAPAN AIRLINES*, n.d.).

Hokkaido Wildlife Park

Situated in the charming city of Sapporo, the Hokkaido Wildlife Park houses a diverse range of animals that are native to the region.

Some of these include deer, foxes, and eagles. You can explore the park at your own pace while learning about Hokkaido's unique ecosystem.

Kushiro Shitsugen National Park

Kushiro Shitsugen National Park, Japan's largest wetland, is an exciting place for avid bird watchers and nature lovers.

It harbors endangered species such as the Japanese crane. Here, alongside the Japanese crane, various waterfowl, raptors, and mammals like red foxes and Hokkaido deer, are also found.

Key Takeaways

- Hokkaido is the northernmost island located in Japan.

- It is known for its mesmerizing beauty and cultural heritage.

- Apart from being home to superb winter-based activities, it has captivating landscapes and lakes, too.

- Hokkaido's wildlife is unlike any other in all of Japan.

CHAPTER 8

Hiroshima and Peace Memorial

Hiroshima means "Wide Island" in Japanese. It is the city of Japan famous for being targeted by the first atomic bomb ever. It originated as a castle place on the delta coastline, on Honshu Island. The city is well-known for its humbleness, food and painful past. This chapter showers light on its devastated past. And the struggles of the native people.

Historical Significance Of Hiroshima

The place where Hiroshima exists today was a small village close to the bay back in the day. This village was cohorted to Buddhist Temple, Mikati-ji. It is believed that this temple was the reason behind Hiroshima's success in the past. During its imperial reign the city was flying towards the sky. It shifted the Japanese economy from rural to urban and became an industrial hub of the country. The city was involved in major historical wars like the Sino-Japanese, Russo-Japanese, and World War I. During this time, it became a pivot of military activity, handled armor, and emerged on the Allied side for these wars.

Fate turned during World War II when Germany surrendered to the allied forces. The war remained in effect in Asia, where the forces stood against the Japanese Reing. This is when the atomic bombing took place. Hiroshima was performing significant shipping of military supplies at that time. And also was the Headquarters for Second General Army and Chūgoku Regional Army. The main military branches that were taking part in World War II ("Hiroshima - Wikipedia," n.d.).

Japan was soaked in destruction and demolition as major cities like Tokyo were bombed. Countless innocent people died and the city was in ruins. Hiroshima was not raided upon yet however, a threat was sensed. People began to seek refuge under the demolished remains of the buildings, and started planning for defense. On Monday, August 6, 1945, at 8:15 am American forces dropped the nuclear bomb "Little Boy " in the center of the city. Most of it was pulled down and spoiled. About 70,000 civilians lost their lives at the time of the bombing. The effects of the nuclear weapon dropped by United States Army Air forces (USAAF), continued till the end of the year. And 90,000 to 166,000 died due to the radiation caused by the blast.

In the coming years, residents of Hiroshima faced negative consequences. There were higher incidences of leukemia, thyroid, breast, and other cancers. Pregnant women were

exposed to greater risks of miscarriages and stillborn babies. Disabilities among newborns have become very common (ICAN, 2017).

World Heritage Sites

The city is home to two of the most significant world heritage sites covered by UNESCO. They are the Hiroshima Peace Memorial Hall and the Itsukushima Shrine. The shine holds great respect for the natives of Japan. It is built on water and is one of the most attractive sceneries to visit in Hiroshima, Japan. It was designated as a World Heritage site in 1996 and has been a place for ancient rituals and ceremonies since then. When in Hiroshima, a visit to the Atomic Bomb Dome cannot be missed. The only remnants left after the explosion were of the Genbaku Dome. The people of Japan kept the shape and structure of the dome preserved afterwards. They put significant efforts to save what remained of it. To this day, it reminds us of the terrific events of 1945. Not only this but it also symbolizes hope and rejoicing all over the world. Hiroshima showcases the struggle and efforts of the Japanese. It displays the fact that the country rebuilt itself rather than kneeling in the face of higher power ("World Heritage," n.d.).

Rebuilding And Resilience

The city was barely recognizable after this terrible incident took place. It was really difficult to rebuild the remains starting from zero. But gradually people stood up. Power, water sources, banks, police stations, and other such managements were made about 30% available. Further improvements were made under the Hiroshima Peace Memorial City Construction Law 1949. Also, a two-year project by the name " Hiroshima Reconstruction And Peacebuilding Research Project " was started. These inventories aided the city with financing and reconstruction. They also helped the people to regain the beloved land they lost as a result of the explosion. The educational, medical, and social services were delivered to people. This maneuver helped the survivors of the atomic attack to get strong emotionally and psychologically.

To this day, the city drowned in ashes, making itself into a developing center point in the world's cane froth. The people remained resilient and worked towards the eradication of the aftereffects of the blast. Now, Japan has appeared again on the world map as an industrial democratic state. It enjoys the freedom of regular elections and forming its own government. It has emerged as a stronger ally than before ("Story of Cities #24: How Hiroshima Rose from the Ashes of Nuclear Destruction | Cities | the Guardian," n.d.).

Initiatives For Promotion Of Peace

Despite such tremendous breakdown, Hiroshima took measures to alleviate nuclear weapon usage all over the world. Their steps to preserve the Atomic Bomb Dome in its actual form after the explosion was one of the first initiatives in this regard. Following maneuvers were made to reduce nuclear weapon usage in the world

- Exhibitions were held wherever needed to spread awareness regarding damage and harm caused by atomic power.

- Posters, planners, and exhibitions were promoted for spreading the news about peace and tranquility in the world.

- Courses were developed for the Hiroshima and Nagasaki Peace Memorial.

- The aftereffects of war were communicated at international levels. This was to reflect on the damage and destruction caused by nuclear bombing.

- The stories of survivors were documented to depict the actual picture of war ("Promoting Initiatives for the Abolition of Nuclear Weapons - 広島市公式ホームページ | 国際平和文化都市," n.d.).

Key Takeaways

Hiroshima was the first victim of an atomic bomb in the world. It suffered great demolition.

- It has two main UNESCO World Heritage sites. The Hiroshima Peace Memorial Hall and Itsukushima Island.

- The city gradually conquered to be a developmental state again.

- It promotes peace and disapproves of using nuclear weapons.

CHAPTER 9

Nara's Cultural Immersion

Nara is the main cultural heritage of Japan. It is the capital of Nara prefecture, located in Japan's Kansai region. Its beauty reflects the ancient shrines, traditional connection and the wild deer carelessly roaming around the region. Dive in deep to know more about this charming city of Japan.

Ancient Temples

Nara paints a magnificent picture of Japanese history, architecture, and evolution. The city is filled with bounties and satisfaction in the form of Shinto shrines, Buddhist temples, and breathtaking landscapes. You can visit the famous excavated site, where once the Great Imperial Palace of Nara stood. The ancient palace depicts the crucial political and developmental period of the country. At that time, Nara kept emerging as the fountainhead of Japan and enjoyed great affluence. To date, it is one of the most famous world heritage sites covered by UNESCO.

History in this part of the country has deep roots. The city has major temples and archaeological buildings showcasing the religion, spirituality and life of the people of Japan. It takes you back to the 8th century when the country was on a ride to prosperity.

Of all the places in Japan, you must attend the majestic temples in Nara. These include some of the most alluring and patronizing buildings, like the Tôdai-ji, kôfuku-ji, Yakushi- ji, and the Gangô-ji temples. These buildings practice utter Buddhism and help you attain pure insight into the religious lessons they offer. Among these Tôdai-ji is considered one of the oldest and the largest temples in East Japan. The Daibutsu-suma, or the statue of "The Great Buddha", is present here. Associated with it, is the Tôdai Museum which is a must-visit also.

Adding onto the beauty, there is Kasuga-Taisha, a Shinto shrine. Also called the Kasuga Grand Shrine, it offers four different deities for visitors to pray. It is the embodiment of offering peace and comfort to those who pay their respects here.

Located behind the Grand Shrine, is the cultural landscape of Kasugayama Primeval Forest. It has been protected by the Kasuga shrine for years and blends nature into your soul ("5 Must-Visit Nara Temples and Shrines: Discover the Timeless Beauty of Japan's Ancient Capital | LIVE JAPAN Travel Guide," n.d.).

Tôdai-ji   kófuku-ji

Yakushi-ji   Gangô-ji

Kasuga-Taisha

Deer Park

One of the most prominent places to visit in Nara is its deer park. You can witness wildlife deer seemingly roaming around the place. They are friendly and harmless and might let you pet them when relaxed. The people of Japan render these creatures sacred and important to them. They are considered majestic and a must for when ancient rituals and ceremonies are being performed. Their participation in yearly events like antler cutting or deer calling ceremonies is always invited with great pleasure and affection ("4 Facts about the Deer of Nara | Nara Travelers Guide," n.d.).

There is a legend about the significance of the deer that dates back to 768 A.D. According to this, the first out of the four Gods of Kasuga-Taisha reached Mikasa in Nara from north of Tokyo on a white deer. After that, the deer became sacred and their killing was met with punishment in the form of death ("Nara's Sacred Deer," n.d.).

The city has a characteristic and unique feature of shunting nature within its culture. You can experience solace and comfort around Mother Nature. It deeply touches your inner

self and blesses you spiritually. This interaction between natural creatures and cultural heritage in the heart of the city is quite peaceful.

Traditional Arts

Apart from all this, the city is an embodiment of traditional arts and crafts. The artistic legacy can be witnessed in ancient tapestries and archaeological buildings. The city enjoys grants to traditional arts and activities like pottery making, calligraphy and sculpture making. The city is known for its Akahada ware pottery from kilns in Yamato Koriyama and itself. The creamy blend of white and red clay, bearing subtle pictures is counted as their unique feature. Production of vases, water pots, fire pots and other earthenware is common among these. On the other hand, calligraphy, along with calligraphy brush making is very profound in this part of the country. The calligraphy is defined, and angled and looks appealing to the eyes. The brushes used for the calligraphy and painting are specially prepared. They are made with kneaded fur from ten different animals. The bristles are extremely fine and give a smooth finish.

One of the most prevalent arts in Nara is sculpture making or sumi. It is a well-known and well-appreciated branch of crafting in Japan. Even the, depicts sculpting skills. The city has countless such sculptures and monuments ("Traditional Crafts of Nara," 2020).

Interestingly, the city offers live workshops and hands-on many traditional activities. You can indulge in different activities and gain pleasurable experiences from them. For instance, there are various accessible cafes and shops where you can try out pottery, calligraphy or traditional washi paper making for the first time in your lives. Places like Fukunishi Washi Honpo, Isshindo, or Yu Nakagawa are major tourist attractions in this respect (Nara, 2016).

Key Takeaways

- Nara is home to various temples and shrines where you can witness the upbringing of their culture and religion.

- The deer moving around freely gives you a feeling of purity and connects you with nature.

- You can enrich yourselves with hands-on experience in certain traditional arts and crafts the city offers.

CHAPTER 10

Must-Try Restaurants Across Japan

Introduction to Japan's Culinary Landscape

In spite of the fact that Japan is known for its outstanding culinary experiences, the country as a whole offers a very stunning and varied selection of cuisine throughout its many locations. There is a wide variety of restaurants in every city, ranging from those that serve street food to those that have earned Michelin stars. Each city also has its own cuisines and specializations. In this chapter, we will examine, via a variety of recommendations, where the best restaurants in the area are located, as well as which location is best for learning about the many types of culinary styles. In the event that you have a preference for sushi, ramen, tempura, or any other dish that this Eastern nation has to offer, then you will undoubtedly discover this guide to be of great assistance in locating the most distinctive dining joints in Japan.

Tokyo

Some of the best restaurants in the world can be found in Tokyo. *Sukiyabashi Jiro*, a three- Michelin-starred sushi restaurant in Ginza known for Jiro Ono's superb creations, is one such location. Although reservations must be made months in advance, this is an unmatched experience. Aoyama's *Narisawa* serves creative Japanese food with an emphasis on sustainability. The cuisine of Chef Yoshihiro Narisawa combines French and Japanese cooking methods with organic products to provide a distinctive eating experience. *Ramen Street* at Tokyo Station is a must-see for ramen enthusiasts. Many highly regarded ramen restaurants, including *Rokurinsha* and *Ikaruga*, can be found in this underground food court. Each restaurant offers a unique twist on the popular noodle soup.

Tempura from *Tempura Kondo* in Ginza is well known for being delicate and cooked to perfection. With great care and attention to detail, the chef makes sure that every piece is flavorful, crispy, and light. *Den* in Jingumae offers a contemporary take on the customary kaiseki (multi-course) meal.

Diners will have a fantastic time at Den thanks to Chef Zaiyu Hasegawa's imaginative and humorous cuisine. Another one not to miss is **Sushi Saito**, a three-Michelin- starred sushi restaurant in Roppongi. The sushi there is frequently compared to perfection on a plate. Last but not least, **Ichiran Ramen** in Shibuya provides a distinctive eating experience with single dining booths that let customers concentrate entirely on their ramen for a more laid-back but no less tasty choice.

Kyoto

Japan's cultural center, Kyoto, is renowned for its sophisticated and beautiful food. Gion's upscale kaiseki restaurant **Kikunoi** serves exquisite dishes that showcase the

greatest ingredients of the season. Each dish is a piece of art. Kikunoi's historical importance contributes to its attraction. The greatest handmade udon noodles in Kyoto can be found at **Omen**, which is close to Ginkakuji. The restaurant is well-liked by both residents and visitors due to its classic atmosphere and delicious food. **Ganko Sushi** in Pontocho provides fresh seafood and sushi prepared in the Kyoto manner, and customers may take in the picturesque views of the Kamogawa River while dining. This is a true sushi experience.

Kyoto speciality sabazushi, or mackerel sushi, is served at **Izuju** in Gion. This venerable restaurant offers a window into the rich gastronomic past of Kyoto. If you're in the mood for something sweet, **Tsujirihei Honten** in Uji is well-known for its matcha-based tea and pastries. Finally, Gion's **Ramen**

Muraji is a little restaurant renowned for its savory and distinctive ramen. It's recommended to arrive early to ensure a position because there is limited seating. **Nishiki Market**, often known as "Kyoto's Kitchen," is another place worth mentioning. Here, guests may indulge in a broad range of regional specialties from a multitude of little merchants.

Osaka

There's good reason why Osaka is sometimes referred regarded as Japan's kitchen. Legendary **Dotonbori Street Food** is served by merchants selling savory okonomiyaki (pancakes) from spots like **Mizuno** and delectable takoyaki (octopus balls) from booths like **Kukuru**. Dotonbori's **Mizuno** is well-known for its okonomiyaki, which is produced using a family recipe that has been passed down through the years. Due to its popularity, the restaurant gets busy frequently, so make plans in advance. Namba's **Ichiran Ramen** provides a special eating experience with its single dining booths, which let customers concentrate just on their ramen. You must sample the delicious tonkotsu broth.

In Tenjinbashi-suji, **Harukoma Sushi** serves excellent sushi at reasonable costs. Popular among the locals, it's renowned for its plentiful and fresh servings. A food lover's dream come true, **Kuromon Ichiba Market** has everything from grilled meats to fresh seafood. It's a must-visit because of the vibrant market atmosphere and extensive culinary selection. Fresh and delectable crab delicacies are the specialty of **Kani Doraku**, which has a famous moving crab sign. At **Zauo** in Dotonbori, patrons may catch their own fish from the restaurant's tanks situated around the dining area and have it cooked to their specifications, making for a very unique eating experience. In every way, this interactive eating experience is enjoyable and novel.

Hokkaido

The northernmost island of Japan, Hokkaido, is well known for its fresh fish. Located in a historic structure, **Sapporo Beer Garden** is well-known for its Genghis Khan BBQ, which is a lamb barbecue combined with local beers. **Otaru's Sushi-dokoro Arashiyama** serves some of Hokkaido's freshest sushi, and the restaurant's lovely

waterfront views enhance the eating experience. Sapporo's **Ramen Shingen** is well-known for its miso ramen, a filling and aromatic meal that is ideal for the chilly Hokkaido weather.

King crab meals are the specialty of Sapporo's **Kani Honke**, for those who adore crab. The restaurant is well-liked because of its large menu and classic decor. Hokkaido's distinctive soup curry, a tasty meal that blends curry spices with fresh, regional ingredients, is served at **Soup Curry GARAKU** in Sapporo. Another highlight is the restaurant **Katsukanino Hanasaki**, which serves a variety of crab delicacies and guarantees a seafood feast to remember. Popular conveyor belt sushi restaurant **Nemuro Hanamaru** provides enjoyable eating together with fresh and reasonably priced sushi.

Hiroshima

The layered, savory pancake known as "okonomiyaki" is a specialty of Hiroshima. The multi-story Okonomimura building, often called Okonomiyaki Village, is home to several okonomiyaki vendors, each of which puts a distinctive twist on the well-loved meal. Reputable okonomiyaki restaurant **Mitchan Sohonten** in Hatchobori is well- known for its tasty combinations and large quantities. If you want to try real okonomiyaki made in the Hiroshima tradition, you have to go there.

With stunning garden views, **Shukkeien Garden Cafe** provides a tranquil eating experience. Fresh ingredients and regional delicacies may be found on the seasonal menu. With a range of fresh,

grilled, and fried oyster meals, **Ekohiiki** in Hiroshima is a popular destination for oyster enthusiasts. The freshest seafood is guaranteed by the restaurant's seasonal menu. Another well-liked okonomiyaki restaurant in Hiroshima is **Nagataya**, which is renowned for its real tastes and lively ambiance. It's a popular among both residents and visitors, so expect a wait. **Sushitei Hikarimachi** offers another distinctive eating experience with freshly made sushi presented in a classy environment with faultless service.

Culinary Exploration Through Cooking Classes

While in Japan, try your best to indulge and take part in the Japanese culture and one of the best ways to do that is by participating in cooking classes that are given by local chefs there in Japan. Trying the hands-on approach will help you learn more and give you the experience of a lifetime. Not to mention the skills that you will learn like the art of rolling sushi.

Gastronomic Adventures Across the Country

From Michelin star restaurants to street food, make the best of your trip by exploring everything. Sampling food is a must when in Japan, and here are a few of the places that you can't miss out on (VisitLaos.org, 2024).

- ▪ **Kunsei Kitchen:** One of the most famous smokehouses in Osaka on the 33rd floor with a dazzling view.

- **Whiskey Nova Steakhouse:** Made on the 32nd floor this restaurant has delectable taste.

- **Smoke & Spin:** Made on the roof-top enjoy the starlight and a delicious meal altogether.

Key Takeaways

- **Tokyo:** Visit Sukiyabashi Jiro for sushi, Narisawa for innovative cuisine, and Ramen Street for diverse ramen options.

- **Kyoto:** Try Kikunoi for kaiseki, Omen for udon, and Izuju for sabazushi.

- **Osaka:** Don't miss Dotonbori for street food, Ichiran Ramen for a unique ramen experience, and Zauo for a fun interactive dining adventure.

- **Hokkaido:** Enjoy Sapporo Beer Garden's BBQ, Sushi-dokoro Arashiyama's sushi, and Soup Curry GARAKU's unique curry.

- **Hiroshima:** Experience Okonomimura for okonomiyaki, Ekohiiki for oysters, and Shukkeien Garden Cafe for a serene dining atmosphere.

CHAPTER 11

Nightlife and Entertainment in Japan

Just as the sun sets down in the Land of the Rising Sun, it welcomes something far beyond its scenic landscapes, iconic places, and bustling city streets.

A new world awakens that offers its people a myriad of experiences that throb with energy and creativity. From the neon lit streets of Tokyo, to the historic pathways of Kyoto, Japan's nightlife and entertainment beckons you with open arms.

Undoubtedly, Japan welcomes you to a varied nightlife and entertainment scene, catering to a wide range of tastes and preferences.

Step into the dazzling lights, bewitching sounds, and enticing flavors that will keep you coming for more!

Tokyo's Neon Playground

Tokyo, Japan's full of life capital, is a city that never truly sleeps. Excitement pulses through its neon-lit-verins, offering an experience for each person unlike no other.

Let's take a stroll through two districts that are particularly known for the diverse nightlife entertainment options they provide. These areas attract both the locals and tourists.

If you are visiting Japan, you need to see both Shinjuku and Shibuya!

Shinjuku

Shinjuku is one of the most accessible areas in the city. Thanks to the JR Shinjuku Station, known to be one of the busiest in the world, it is one of the easiest stations to navigate your way across (*Shinjuku: The Heart of Tokyo's Nightlife and Entertainment*, 2024).

As dusk descends, the streets of Shinjuku come alive with a variety of neon lights, drawing you into the world of sensory delights.

Stopping by a place called Golden Gai, you might get lost in the narrow, busy streets. These alleyways are crammed with cozy izakayas that offer cold beers and sizzling yakitori skewers.

With its unique charm, amidst the chatter of the locals and grilling of meat, you'll get to witness the true essence of Tokyo's nightlife culture.

Shibuya

Shibuya, the destination where both fashion and chaos collide! A neon-lit district, this area promises you an irresistible sensory overload of symphony of sights, sounds, and smells.

You'll find this area buzzing with enigmatic youthful energy, where you can also indulge yourself in retail therapy. It's home to places such as the famous Shibuya Crossing, and the pretty streets of Dogenzaka and Udagawacho.

Shibuya is known for its vibrant nightlife, offering a diverse range of bars and clubs. Here are some of the best spots to check out:

1. **Womb A club** is known for its top notch DJs, excellent sound, and a large dance floor; Womb is one of the most popular night clubs in Tokyo. Its 'techno' look and energized environment put it on most people's list when they are out hunting for a wild night.

2. **Hobgoblin** For the lovers of British pub culture Hobgoblin provides warm atmosphere and choice of beers and traditional pub food. The pub offers live music and screening of sports events allowing patrons to enjoy their time in a casual manner.

3. **Geronimo Shot Bar** Being a local bar Geronimo Shot Bar boasts a variety of shots and cocktails as well as become a favorite among the tourists. It has the right atmosphere for a friendly place to have a few drinks, especially there is usually music playing and people are usually quite cheerful.

4. **Shibuya Sky Lounge** Shibuya Sky Lounge is a view deck and the special bar where the service is situated on the top floor of the Shibuya Scramble Square building, so the guests can enjoy the perfect view of the city from there. It is ideal for contemporary and stylish cocktail accompanied by a view of the city lights.

5. **Tusk Tusk** is a posh club with a contemporary art deco design with vintage outlook, and cozy ambiance. It boasts about wonderful interiors, an excellent choice of alcoholic beverages and some truly good music list, which gives the place quite a sophisticated air of a go-to club for a classy evening.

6. **Karaoke Kan** Again for a more entertaining night out at Shibuya, Karaoke Kan which offers enclosed karaoke rooms where friends can sing to the best of their voices. The venue also has various drinks and snacks available that are perfect to enjoy while you sing along to your favorite tunes.

7. **Club Camelot** Club Camelot This is a popular nightclub that has numerous floors with different sections for different types of music and moods. Opened to popular dancing and revelry, it's ideal for people who are in search of special events.

8. **The Room** The Room is an underground club based on its enhanced small dancing area and famous music style. With a focus on house and techno, it gives customers a more relaxed take on the traditional concept of clubbing.

9. **Bar Quest** Bar Quest is an extravagant cocktail bar famous for artworks on many of its signature cocktails and adult themes. It is suitable for those

who would like to try out some delicious cocktail in a chic, but not posh atmosphere.

You'll get to adventure through an array of stylish rooftop bars, clubs, restaurants, tailored for anyone's specific needs.

Shibuya is famous for its lively music scene, hosting both local and international artists in various venues. From rock to jazz, there's music for every taste (*Tokyo Nightlife: Shibuya Vs. Roppongi - Trip To Japan*, 2024).

Apart from that, there are other entertainment options that won't give you the chance to sulk or get bored.

Osaka's Dynamic Night Scene

Whether you are in the mood for a casual drink, dancing to the local DJ beats, or simply want to experience the iconic nightlife in Japan, Osaka has it all!

If you want to find the perfect place to dance the night away, you need to know about Bar Nayuta. Step into this beloved cocktail spot that is adored by both the locals and tourists because of its warm ambiance (*Osaka Nightlife & Party Guide – 2024*, 2024).

You'll witness skilled bartenders pitch in the delicious cocktails using top notch ingredients, and unwavering spirits.The friendly staff here will guide you through if you are unable to place an order.

Nonetheless, you can find various other options such as Giraffe Osaka in Dotombori, Club Joule in America Village (Americamura), and Sam and Dave One near Souemoncho in Shinsaibashi!

Coastal Extravaganza in Yokohama

Yokohama, a city located along Japan's Pacific coastline, is one of the country's 15 designated government cities.

The total population spikes to 3.7 million, making it the second largest city after Tokyo. Thanks to its strategic location, Yokohama boasts a thriving international trading port, attracting numerous foreign enterprises (*About Yokohama | Yokohama Official Visitors Guide - Travel Guide to Yokohama City*, n.d.).

It's not just a tourist hotspot; Yokohama offers a full range of urban functions, from business to culture. It's a city of dreams for both locals and visitors alike.

Coastal evenings in Yokohama welcome you to a unique blend of relaxation and excitement. You can explore seafront parks like Yamashita Park and Rinko Park, perfect for a leisurely picnic or romantic stroll.

For a livelier vibe, head to the bustling Minato Mirai district, where waterfront clubs, trendy bars, and chic restaurants await. Indulge in delicious seafood or sip cocktails while soaking in the city lights from a rooftop bar.

As the night unfolds, you can join beachside parties and outdoor events along the coast!

Yokohama

Kyoto's Magical Evenings

Enter Kyoto, where, with every enchanting evening, ancient tradition meets the modern allure. You'd love to explore the historic streets and cultural wonders.

Discover the iconic Gion district, where the lantern-lit pathways and traditional machiya houses evoke the sense of old-world charm. Here, you may even come across geisha, eloquently gliding through the streets, adding to the district's timeless image.

For a perfect day in Kyoto, pair your visit to Gion with a leisurely stroll through the charming Higashiyama District. Wander between Yasaka Shrine and Kiyomizudera Temple, where you'll find beautifully preserved streets lined with traditional shops, and local foods, crafts, and souvenirs (*Gion - Kyoto Travel*, 2022).

Along the heavenly banks of River Kamogawa, get a chance to see elegant dances and beguiling music. These traditional performances narrate the tale of Kyoto's rich cultural heritage.

Island Vibes in Okinawa

Okinawa, is Japan's very own tropical heaven, recounted for its stellar beaches, rich culture, and profound history.

Did you know? Okinawans have less cancer, heart disease, and dementia than Americans, and women there live longer than any women on the planet (*Okinawa, Japan*, n.d.).

Nonetheless, Okinawa's nightlife has always been vibrant, reflecting its status as a trade hub. At local Izakayas, enjoy all-you-can-eat and all-you-can-drink specials.

Don't miss local drinks like Orion beer and awamori rice wine. You can also check out The Dojo Bar for a unique experience, and Parker's Mood Jazz Club for a refined setting with fine wine and music.

You'd also get to experience Okinawa's nightlife in full swing with cocktails and local drinks at beachfront bars featuring live music and DJs. In addition, you can watch mesmerizing fire shows on the beach and laid-back reggae vibes at beach bars.

Lastly, you cannot forget about the beach parties! Witness live music, games, bonfires, and a lively atmosphere drawing locals and visitors!

Here are some of the best beach bars in Okinawa where you can enjoy stunning views, delicious drinks, and a relaxed atmosphere:

1. **Kiki's Beach Bar** (Naha) Located near Naha's waterfront, Kiki's Beach Bar offers a laid-back vibe with fantastic ocean views. Enjoy tropical cocktails, fresh seafood, and a casual setting perfect for unwinding after a day on the beach.

2. **Beachside Cafe Tida** (Onna) Situated right on the beach, Beachside Cafe Tida provides a relaxed atmosphere with beautiful sunset views. Savor a variety of drinks, including tropical cocktails and local craft beers, while enjoying the serene beach environment.

3. **Kume Island Beach Bar** (Kumejima) This beach bar on Kume Island features a relaxed, island-inspired atmosphere with stunning ocean views. Enjoy a range of cocktails, light bites, and a tranquil setting perfect for sunset watching.

4. **Blue Seal Ice Cream and Beach Bar** (Mihama) Located in the American Village area, this beach bar combines a fun atmosphere with Blue Seal's famous ice cream. It's a great spot to enjoy a refreshing drink or ice cream treat while relaxing by the beach.

5. **Hama Ryu** (Chatan) Located in the Chatan area, Hama Ryu offers a beachside bar experience with a focus on fresh seafood and tropical drinks. The casual setting and proximity to the water make it a great place to enjoy a relaxed meal and drinks.

Key Takeaways

- Tokyo, Japan's neon capital, offers various entertainment options, and a memorable nightlife. With cozy izakayas, and eatery options, expect an all rounder display.

- Immerse yourself in Osaka's savory cocktails, and local nightclubs for your party scenes.

- Enjoy coastal evenings and a unique blend of excitement in Yokohama.

- Discover Kyoto's Gion District, where a lantern-lit path awaits you.

- Get island vibes no better than in Okinawa. Attend beach parties and tune in to lively music that would leave you in a state of euphoria.

CHAPTER 12

Onsen Retreats in Beppu

If this is your first time traveling to Japan, then you must not be aware of the term *"onsen"* until now.

Simply put, the onsen is referred to as the Japanese hot springs and the facilities that surround them. These natural baths are adored for relaxation, and the health benefits they offer due to their mineral content (*What Is Onsen(Hot Spring) ?*, n.d.).

Nevertheless, let's get into the serene onsen retreats that Beppu offers! Stay rest assured, you won't be found any better than the ones experienced here by locals and visitors too.

Soaking In Hot Springs

Beppu's hot springs have been called the therapeutic ones for one can enjoy a variety. This is Beppu's main attraction; to be able to enjoy such types in a small town.

When people think of onsens, they just think of bathing in natural hot springs. However, Japanese people have an altered art of enjoying this phenomena they have always been in company with.

Let's discover some of the types of onsens each offering unique benefits for relaxation and rejuvenation.

Hells Onsen

Experience the mysterious and temperamental springs of Beppu.

Best known as the Seven Hells of Beppu, it's the collection of colorful and geothermally active hot springs with temperatures too high for bathing (*Hells of Beppu | Travel Japan*, n.d.).

These quaint, natural wonders display vibrant hues and bubbling waters, providing a visual treat while you explore their surroundings.

Mineral Rich Waters

Indulge in onsens that are filled with mineral-rich waters. These are believed to offer multitudinous health benefits.

These provide a wellness experience unlike no other. They specialize in relieving muscle tension and fatigue, as well as skin improvements.

These soothing onsens should be number one on your list, if you are looking to unwind the physical and mental ache of your body.

Warm Sand Bath

One of the traditional onsens is the Suna-yu. In this type of onsen, the heat of the hot spring is used to heat the sand.

For this, one is buried in naturally heated sand to promote relaxation and detoxification. Fret not, this sand is clean, as it is washed consistently.

As you lie down, the staff covers you with the sand until your neck (your face is left uncovered), and 10 minutes are provided to unwind.

During this, your body gradually releases heat from its core, providing a deeply relaxing experience (*The Rarest Onsen in Japan?! The "Sunayu" Feature Article - Enjoy Onsen*, 2018).

Mud Bath

Want to rejuvenate your dull skin? Beppu's mud baths are just what you are looking for!

These mud baths, also known as Doro-yu, are a rare sight. The steam from the onsen combines with clay in the earth, enriching it with mineral water and creating a mud bath.

This unique blend contains concentrated minerals sought after in onsen experiences. It utilizes mineral-rich mud to cleanse and nourish the skin. The therapeutic properties of the mud help detoxify the body and promote a sense of well-being.

Beppu Hoyo Land Onsen is a renowned destination where you can indulge in this exceptional mud bath experience (*Hot Springs Are Not Just For Bathing?! Four Other Ways To Enjoy Onsen - Enjoy Onsen*, 2018).

Wellness and Relaxation

In addition to the onsens in Beppu, Japan, there are other options to look out for and experience while on your trip. A wellness retreat sounds like the most dreamy getaway from our hustling and bustling lives.

Explore the wellness resorts and relaxation options in Beppu. They offer the ideal blend of traditional spa treatments and modern wellness practices for a refreshing experience.

You can indulge in the luxury of private spa retreats, offering exclusive access to onsen baths and personalized treatments.

Whether it's a serene outdoor onsen overlooking scenic landscapes or a tranquil indoor spa sanctuary, these private retreats provide an intimate thrill.

Modern wellness techniques such as aromatherapy massages, meditation classes, and yoga routines are offered at certain wellness resorts. These also involve traditional Japanese techniques with contemporary wellness methods for a holistic approach.

One of the greatest things about Japan is its food. Nourish your body with healthy and delicious cuisine, featuring locally sourced ingredients known for their nutritional benefits (Zerkalenkov, 2022).

Many wellness retreats in Japan provide vegan or vegetarian options to ensure you receive all the essential nutrients your body requires.

Exploring the Town

Aside from the reposing onsens and wellness resorts, the town has a lot to offer itself!

Lose yourself in the addicting flavors of Beppu by trying out local specialties such as jigoku-mushi cuisine, where food is steamed using the natural geothermal heat from the "Hells" of Beppu.

One of the most charming experiences you can have in Beppu is steaming your own food by the hot springs. Aside from the stunning bathing activity, there is a cooking delight waiting to be explored.

Visit Jigoku Mushi Kobo where you can select fresh ingredients to steam. The hot steam from the nearby hot springs quickly cooks your food (*15 Awesome Things To Do In Beppu In 2024 | Travel Guide*, n.d.).

Beppu's charming shopping districts welcome you to browse for unique souvenirs and local handicrafts.

You can visit traditional markets such as Beppu Onsenji Shopping Street to take back memories of your trip. You can also shop for artisanal goods, pottery, and regional delicacies to alleviate your experience.

Don't forget to visit attractions such as Beppu Park if you are looking to take a casual stroll through the middle of the city.

You can also enjoy the fresh scent of pine trees and the ever-changing colors of native flowers. Get away from the city's crowds, featuring vibrant flowerbeds and towering bamboo groves (Brown, n.d.).

During cherry blossom season, don't miss the park's stunning display of delicate blooms!

Beppu

Key Takeaways

- Beppu is the perfect destination to experience Japanese hot springs (onsens) and its various types.

- Luxury spas, yoga, meditation, and mouth-watering food options are out there to discover.

- Shopping areas are full of traditional souvenirs to take back home from your trip.

- Visit parks and other attractions to walk along the many things Beppu has to offer.

CHAPTER 13

Island Adventures in Okinawa

Japan, a country that has so much to offer and explore, is one of the best places for you to visit. And when we talk about all that Japan has to offer, how can we forget about the incredible adventures that Okinawa has to offer you that will make your trip one of the best.

In this chapter we will be discussing all the amazing activities and adventures that Okinawa offers. So what are we waiting for? Lets jump right in, or more like dive right in.

Tropical Beaches

If you think that the list of reasons why you should visit Japan is coming to an end, you will be disappointed. We have already talked about the nightlife and many other unforgettable experiences that Japan has to offer, but how can we forget the pristine beaches that Japan has? Let me just paint a picture in your head: imagine yourself lying on soft sand as you soak up the sun and stare at the turquoise water stretching farther than you can see as you enjoy the soft ocean breeze. Sounds like the best way to spend your vacation, doesn't it?

Okinawa offers some of the most beautiful and mesmerizing beaches that make you feel like you are in heaven. When you visit Okinawa, you will find that many of its main and outlying islands are made into swimming beaches that are not only breathtaking but also have amenities available for visitors and are open all year round.

Here is a list of beaches present in the central and south of Okinawa that you can visit (Official Okinawa Travel Guide, 2024):

1. Zanpa Beach

Famous for its white powdery sand and crystal-clear water, this beach is the perfect retreat for you. Since it is a beach made for swimming, you will find that it also has other activities that you might like to try like snorkeling and exploring the marine life.

2. Narai Beach

Another breathtaking spot that you must visit on your trip to Japan is the Narai Beach, which is situated on the Southern Coast of Miyako Island, that offers the best water adventure and offers you a chance to explore the vibrant and captivating underwater world that exists beneath those crashing waves of glittery turquoise water. A small tip for the people going there for the first time is to never give up on a chance to go snorkeling. There is a whole new world waiting for you down there waiting to be explored.

3. Ikei Beach

Last but not the least is the Ikei Beach that sits upon the Ikei Island in Japan is one of the most exhilarating places that you can visit. The water there is so many shades of blue that you might lose count. This beach also offers an enigmatic experience of beachside dining. Enjoy the freshly caught seafood, filled with Japanese spices and flavors.

Although these three are a few of the best beaches that Okinawa has, remember that there are countless more than you can find with similar activities. Remember that your comfort should be your first priority, so you can always look up beaches that might be closer to you. Your traveling is more about your experience and not the place is something you need to remember.

OKINAWA ISLAND

1 Zanpa Beach

2 Narai Beach

3 Ikea Beach

Traditional Okinawan Culture

Described as the culture of islands, Okinawa is a blend of different cultural practices and traditions. The modern and the ancient traditions merge together seamlessly to bring together the new lifestyle of the Okinawan people. As you embark on your journey to explore Okinawan culture, you will find that the unique cultural heritage is made of a dynamic mix of characteristics that come from various countries like China, Korea, South Asia, and Japan that are all tied together through trade. From the traditional dance to the local way of life, everything is influenced by different cultures. (Japan, 2024)

Okinawa is known for its Classical performing arts, and offers a myriad of art and skill waiting to be explored. Here is a list of things that you must experience on your trip to Okinawa:

1. Ryuki Dance

Categorized into three different kinds of dances:

- Traditional Dance was performed to welcome guests in the Ryukyu Era

- Zo Dance demonstrates the music and the culture of the common people

- Creative Dance is choreographed by modern dancers and is constantly evolving (Japan, 2024).

This dance is performed in costumes, and in the background plays the Sanshin, a three- stringed guitar that is one of the most fundamental parts of Okinawa's performing arts (Accessible Travel Okinawa, n.d.).

2. Kumiodori

It is a musical theater that blends words, music and dance to entertain people. The history behind it also pays tribute to the Ryukyu Kingdom as it was introduced to entertain Chinese envoys that came to crown the King of the Ryukyu Kingdom. Moreover, it was designated a National Important Intangible Cultural Property as one of Japan's superior performing arts.

3. Folk entertainment

The main form of folk entertainment is Eisa and Shishima. Eisa is a dance performance done by the young people of Okinawa during the Bon Festival. These people gather to honor the spirits of their ancestors. While Shishimai, also known as the Lion Dance is yet another favorite. It gained its heritage from China and was done to get rid of evil and pray for better crops and prosperity.

4. Yachimun

A blend of colorful and creative designs used to make pottery that is based on patterns and colors taken from the Okinawa itself pays testimony to both the ocean and the plant life there. (Japan n.d.)

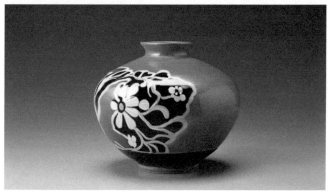

5. Lunar New Year

One of the most celebrated events in Okinawa, using the old calendar it is celebrated at the end of the year typically in February. You will find seasonal items packed with many colorful decorations (Official Okinawa Travel Guide, 2024b).

Historical Sites

Known for its history and heritage there are a series of places you must visit (Google Arts & Culture, n.d.).

1. Shurijo Castle

Also known as the center of Ryukyu Kingdom, it has a lengthy history. It has been burned down several times and still remains standing. It is a mustvisit place due to its architecture.

2. Sonohyan Utaki Ishimon

A stone gate outside a sacred forest is a sight to behold. Built in 1519, it was used as a place for offering prayers for the Ryukyu King and the architecture.

3. Peace Memorial Park

The world war made Okinawa a site of a very bloody battle, and the impact of it can still be seen in this park. It gives an overview of the land and all the destruction that was brought upon it (*War Memorials*, n.d.).

OKINAWA ISLAND

1 Shurijo Castle

2 Sonohyan Utaki Ishimon

3 Peace Memorial Park

CHAPTER 14

Accomodation in Japan

When traveling, one of the biggest concerns that people have is their accommodation. Where to base, how costly it will be, how long should I stay? There are a million things that come to mind when you find yourself looking for a place to stay on your trip. And what makes it even harder is the lack of options.

But luckily, Japan has no such problems. Not only is Japan offering some of the most diverse lodging experiences but it also has a variety that few other countries have. You can find whatever you want in your budget because of the several options that Japan has.

In this chapter we will explore the different options you have and the kind of things you need to keep in mind when finding accommodation.

Diverse Lodging Experiences

After a day of exploring and entertainment, the one thing that you can think of is how great it would be to sink into your bed and let sleep take over you. A basic necessity, and one of the most important details to take care of when traveling is your accommodation.

Your comfort is important, which is why it is best that you look into all the options you have available. Japan has different kinds of accommodations available for you based on your budget. Let's explore a few of those options.

1. Traditional Ryokans in Kyoto

We have already established how delightful the culture of Japan is, and missing out on it won't be a good idea. So, when looking for accommodation, staying at a traditional ryokan is a must. If you haven't heard of them before, let me put it simply: a ryokan is a traditional Japanese inn that is made in Japanese style. I am sure you are wondering, how are they different from hotels? They are. Like the name suggests this place has all the traditional stuff inside. From Tatami mat floors, woven from straw to the kaiseki spread everything there has a true heritage behind it.

When you enter the Ryokan, you are firstly asked to remove your shoes outside, in the foyer before you are shown to your room, which you will find will already have a cup of tea and traditional sweets or crackers waiting for you. After the refreshment, you can choose to shower while a maid lays out your futon.

If you haven't heard of futons before, these are traditional beds that are laid out on tatami mats as people in the old times in Japan had a custom of sleeping on the floor.

And the most important part is the food, which is a whole kaiseki spread filled with Japanese cuisine. Remember that when booking a Ryokan, you will be paying on the per person basis, and while you might think it's expensive, it also has two meals with your stay which makes a great ryokan a three-star residential restaurant (Rowthorn, 2024).

2. Capsule Hotels in Tokyo

Not everyone is the same so if you opt out of the cultural accommodation, you can always choose to go for one of the most modern and successful inventions in Tokyo, which are Capsule Hotels. These hotels were initially made for late workers or people who missed the last bus. But the increased popularity of this accommodation has made it successful.

You can find accommodation in the middle of the city for half the price of a hotel room. And you get more privacy in this room than in any hotel. This hotel offers more than just a regular bed to sleep in. Instead, you get a fancy bed setup that includes a big cinema screen and a bed that can also monitor your body's sleep patterns while you rest (Rakuten Travel, n.d.).

Here are a list of hotels you should try:

- Shinjuku Kuyakusho-mae Capsule Hotel
- Sauna & Capsule Hotel Hokuo
- The Millennials Shibuya

3. Luxury Ryokans in Hakone

If you ever ask a Japanese person, look what comes to his mind when he thinks of Hakone, the first thing they are likely to say is hot springs. We have already discussed what Ryokans are, but the Ryokans in Hakone are that they are surrounded by scenic beauty and onsens, also known as hot springs which make the stay luxurious. Here are a bunch of Ryokans you can try (Sasaki, 2024):

- Natural SPA Auberge gen Hakone Gora
- Hakone Pax Yoshino
- Hotel Hanagokoro

Strategic Locations

While choosing your location there are a few things you need to keep in mind.

1. Proximity to Attractions

Everyday, you will wake up with some kinds of plans to visit the attractions of the city. Imagine having to travel several hours to and from whatever spot you want to visit. That sounds as tiring as it can get, so try to choose your accommodation strategically, and make sure it is located near some common landmark, for example, Inari Shrine or Shibuya Crossing which is in the heart of commotion.

2. Local Neighborhood Immersion

Once you are in Japan, try your best to enjoy the local life the most. That is where you will find the most authentic of experiences. This is why when choosing a place to live you may find that living in a local neighborhood might be fun as it will give you the chance to not only engage with locals but also get a chance to find hidden gems.

3. Transportation Accessibility

Always remember that you are not a local there and the odds of you having your own vehicle are low, hence transportation will be a dire need for you. Always choose accommodation that will have easy access to public transportation hubs. Try living near to train stations or bus terminals.

Varied Accommodation Choices

Once you have an idea of what you are looking for and what your budget is, you will quickly find that Japan has a wide array of options available for everyone. There is a selection of lodging options you can choose from ranging from the most expensive to the cheapest options. Here are some of the options:

1. Luxurious Hotels in Tokyo

Unbeknownst to many, Tokyo offers one of the most eye-catching views and a rich culture followed by some of the most expensive and luxurious hotels in the world that provide you with the best services.

Here are some examples (Sasaki, 2024b):

- Aman Tokyo

- Bulgari Hotel Tokyo

- The Ritz-Carlton Tokyo

2. Quaint Hostels in Kyoto

It's alright if you don't have the budget to book yourself the most luxurious hotel in Tokyo, because there is a great option for you too. For budget-friendly accommodations you can find hostels that fit your every need. Here are a few you can check out:

- Mosaic Hostel Kyoto

- Kyoto Morris Hostel

- K's House Tokyo Oasis

- Grids Tokyo Asakusabashi

3. Airbnb's in Osaka's Local Residences

Last but not the least is your option to Airbnb. Homesickness is a feeling that stops by often while traveling, and Airbnb is the best option for you to experience life at home while being away from home. Not only will this save your money but also give you a chance to live with local Japanese people and learn their culture and lifestyle better.

CHAPTER 15

Photography Hotspots in Japan

What's a traveling experience without any pictures? In today's time there is no one that doesn't want to take pictures to commemorate the moment. And Japan is one of the best places to be photographed in. Japan has a land full of landscapes that leave you gaping and a cultural richness that isn't found in many countries. It doesn't matter if you are an amateur photographer or a professional one, who needs skill when the place's own charm is enough to make the pictures look stunning. So, let's explore some of the places that are a must visit on your trip to Japan.

Captivating Landscapes

There are a bunch of places that you need to visit, but let me just list down a few that are the most popular and worthwhile.

Cherry Blossom Scenes

Also known as Sakura, cherry blossom season is one of the most beautiful seasons in Japan. Delicate and different shades of pink blossom all over the country, blanketing it with a beautiful sight to behold as the parks and streets transform into an enchanting scene that looks like it is straight out of a fairytale.

One of the most important parts of visiting Japan to witness the Cherry Blossom season is to make sure you time your vacation according to the blooming scenes. The peak bloom you will find, varies from year to year, depending on the different kinds of weather. But the average blooming season is spring, from late March to early April. There are annual Sakura forecasts, too that you can use to be on track.

Although there are many parks that you can visit here are two that are the most popular (Xie, 2024):

Tokyo's Ueno Park

This park is one of the most popular tourist attractions in Japan, situated in Tokyo, this park is home to a 1000 cherry blossoms along with many museums, shrines and even ponds. During the blooming season which starts around late March and is *active* for two weeks, you will find it open mostly from 5pm to 9pm.

Kyoto's Maruyama Park

Kyoto, an ancient city of Japan and the capital city, is the heart of the Sakura season. From March till April, you will mostly find this place crowded with people in the Maruyama Park, where an event takes place in which a tall shidarezakura, also known as the weeping cherry tree is lit up at night along with other stunning sights like the Philosopher's Path which is a canal that has hundreds of cherry trees lining it's passage.

Mount Fuji Panoramas

Mount Fuji is yet another sight to behold in this land of sights. It is one of the highest mountains present in Japan. For those of you who don't know, it is a dormant volcano that has been classified as active but hasn't erupted since 1707 (P. Rafferty, 2024). It is best to view the beauty of this place from vantage spots to see it more clearly. You can visit places like:

Chureito Pagoda

This is a five-story pagoda that provides you with an excellent view of Mount Fuji but also the Fujiyoshida City. It is a popular spot for photographers as it allows them some of the most beautiful shots (Chureito Pagoda, n.d.).

Lake Kawaguchi

One of the most easily accessible lakes in the Fuji Five Lakes has one of the best views of Mount Fuji. And the view is even more spectacular in the Sakura season (Japan Guide, n.d.)

Cultural Moments

A country with such a rich cultural heritage needs to be explored and captured. Here are some of the places that are worth getting photographed:

1. Gion's Traditional Atmosphere

One of the historic and most enchanting places in Kyoko's history is the Gion district, where you can still find Japan's past resonating. For anyone interested in exploring Japanese culture this place is a must try. Filled with ancient buildings and quiet streets, this place has a charm of its own that can only be found here. So much so that the power cables here have been put underground to maintain its traditional ambience. Known for the traditional wooden houses called machiya houses and traditional teahouses, this place captures your heart. With alleyways lined with lanterns and geisha, who are skilled performers famous for their skills in traditional art (Live Japan, 2023).

2. Street Scenes in Tokyo

Capital of Japan, Tokyo is the heart of the country that offers a wide range of experiences. And the best way to experience it is in the streets of Tokyo. A tip for explorers there is to shut off their phones and explore the city on your own. A place where the past blends with the present seamlessly, there are a bunch of places you should visit. Starting from the iconic Shibuya Crossing to Nakamise Street, enjoy your time as you go through the neon lights lighting up streets with people swarming around all day.

Historical and Artistic Shots

Explore the timeless beauty of Japan as you go through the cities and find places rich with history and background with stunning views that make you blink just to be sure that you are not dreaming. Here are two places that are very highly recommended by the Japanese locals.

1. Arashiyama Bamboo Grove

Standing in the soaring bamboo stalks lining the path, Arashiyama Bamboo Grove has become one of the most popular places in Japan that pays testimony to the timeless beauty of nature. As you walk through the woods and the little sunlight that passes the trees shines over you, you will feel like you have been transported to a whole new place. It is a good idea to visit a place like this in the early morning or late afternoon to experience the true beauty of this place.

2. Meiji Shrine and Harajuku's Takeshita Street

Last but not the least is the Meiji Shrine, which is hidden behind a forest in the heart of Tokyo. This place is perfect for a peaceful retreat from the hustle and bustle of your everyday life. It is the perfect place for you to visit when you need a break from your daily life as you lose yourself in the winding pathways and the towering torii gates present there.

Not very far from Takeshita Street, which is full of people and vibrant colors. Known for its lively atmosphere, this place serves as the best backdrop with a wide array of colorful shops, cafes and street food stalls that win your heart.

Key Takeaways

- If photographs are one of the most important parts of your trips and Japan is the perfect spot for it.
- Explore the parks that have the best views and scenic beauty to get the perfect shot.
- Remember to indulge in cultural moments that are colorful and lively.
- Don't forget to visit the Shrine and other spots that are famous that are known for their views.

CHAPTER 16

Healthy and Safety in Japan

While having fun and making the best memories is the main takeaway from a trip, you also need to remember that your safety and well-being are a priority. One of the most important tasks before a trip is to make sure you will remain safe and well in the process. Here are a few things that you need to keep in mind when you travel to Japan.

Essential Precautions

Always remember that it is better to be safe than sorry. Here are a few precautions that you must take into consideration before your trip:

Japan-Specific Travel Insurance

This is a crucial part of your traveling experience. It is essential that you have Japan- Specific Travel insurance. Remember that no sickness comes with a warning. Should you get sick or get injured during the trip it will cost you thousands of dollars to get treated which you might not have in your budget. This is why you should consider insurance. This kind of insurance will cover several aspects of your journey like (Auras Insurance, n.d.).

- Medical care

- Loss of documents

- Accidents

- Medical transport services

Health Consultation for Japan Travel

Before leaving for Japan, make sure you check all the health specific advice and get all the vaccinations that are recommended to travel to Japan. It is best to get a routine checkup before you leave so you know for sure that you are in your optimal health condition and there will be no issues while you are traveling. If you have any allergies or respiratory issues, make sure to check the climate and environment in Japan that could potentially trigger your allergies.

Staying Healthy on the Road

You are the most vulnerable when you are out in public, exposed to every kind of germs or disease that might be in the air. It is important to maintain a good hygienic routine to make sure you don't get sick.

Hygiene Practices in Japan

Luckily for you, Japan is a place that values good hygiene practices and has a strong awareness of it. It is customary for these people to wash their hands often and gargle as soon as they come home. Not on this but it is a common norm for them to hop into showers and get clean before they go to bed. For people who come from other countries, this comes as a shock simply because it is not common for countries to have such thorough cleaning rituals. And you should hop right in and join them in these practices when you are there to maintain your health (Web Japan 2020).

Safe Travel Practices in Japan

A tip for all travelers that goes a long way is to always know your surroundings. You need to know your way around the place and know what to do in case of emergencies. People often make the mistake of leaving things like this thinking they will figure it out if the need arises. You never know what you might end up facing and it is best to prepare yourself beforehand to avoid any regrets.

- **Awareness of Japanese Medical Facilities**

The first and foremost thing to do when you find your accommodation is to save a few of the emergency helpline numbers in your phone. You need to familiarize yourself with the location and whatever facilities are being offered to you as a tourist. You can also visit the "Search Medical Institution" site available on the Japan Tourism Agency or check with hotel desks to get help. Even your travel insurance will help guide you in this situation (Live Japan, 2020).

- **Road Safety and Cultural Sensitivity in Japan**

Almost everyone is prone to get into accidents if you aren't careful enough and in a country like Japan. With its bustling crowds, it is a place you need to be careful in. Thankfully Japan has been credited as one of the best traffic safety record nations. Japan

is known for its innovative approach toward transportation, and has recorded fewer than 3000 accidents in 2021, which is a stark comparison between America and Japan. Japanese roads are built safely but there are a few rules that you must conform with when you are there.

One of those rules is no street parking, which makes people there less prone to get into accidents. As well as the usage of minicars which are lightweight and have an absence of stubby front ends that can avoid driver blind spots. And of the most important things you will notice there is that children tend to travel alone there. People mostly credit the culture for this development as they support independence (Bloomberg, 2022).

Preparedness for Japan's Unique Challenges

There are some things that you can predict but most that you can't. but you can always be prepared by keeping up with a country's challenges. From climate change to natural disasters, remember to always be prepared for surprises.

Natural Disaster Readiness in Japan

Unfortunately, Japan has been the target of many natural disasters over the history. It is considered vulnerable to more disasters because of its location and the topography there. It has been subject to many earthquakes, typhoons and other types of natural disasters over the years *(MOFA: Disasters and Disaster Prevention in Japan, n.d.).*

But several measures have been taken to avoid any injuries due to the hazard. You can now use a type of map which is called a hazard map. This invention helps you see all the risk areas for disasters that include overflowing rivers and landslides that you need to avoid to stay safe. You can now see this information on your phones or even PCs for convenience. And you can also find booklets with all kinds of information that you need for disaster prevention in Tokyo that you can use (Web-Japan, n.d.).

Responsible Exploration and Cybersecurity

When you are in Japan there will be countless activities indoors and outdoors that you can participate in. But be sure to practice responsible behavior and only go for activities that offer you the maximum level of safety and the minimum level of risk. And remember to practice cybersecurity precautions by only using secure networks.

All these things are listed above as a precaution. As a whole Japan is one of the most safest places in the world with one of the most welcoming and friendly population across any country in the world. We are sure your experience is going to be just incredible.

Key Takeaways

- Your health should be your biggest priority and it is essential to take precautions on your trip.

- Follow the practices that people in Japan tend to follow to remain healthy and safe.

- Beware of Road Safety and make sure you don't offend the locals there.

- Know about the current situation and the likelihood of disaster in Japan. Make sure you have prepared yourself for every scenario.

CHAPTER 17

Language Tips in Japan

One of the biggest problems when traveling abroad that arises is the language barrier. Though it might not seem like such a big problem while you are still in your own country, you will realize very quickly when you arrive that the language barrier can create quite a few problems in your trip. People struggle the most when they cannot communicate with anyone in a new country, which mostly stresses them out and shoves them to the brink of frustration. And it is crucial to avoid this kind of problem by a few simple steps in which you take out the time and learn just a few things that might make your trip easier.

Essential Japanese Phrases for Daily Communication

On your trip to Japan, it is highly recommended that you get accustomed to some of the daily life sentences that will help you communicate with people more easily. Not only does this help you but it also allows you to interact with the locals there and build a few decent connections and feel less like an outsider. And you won't regret it when you see the genuine happiness and surprise on the local's faces when you speak their language.

Greetings and Polite Expressions

When you start looking for words that you must learn in Japanese you might get sucked into the rabbit hole and to avoid that let me give you a few phrases that you must know (Yoko, 2020):

- Ohayou-gozaimasu = Good morning

- Kon'nichiwa = Hello

- Konbanwa = Good evening

- Arigatou gozaimasu = Thank you

- Hai = Yes

- § Iie = No

- Sumimasen = Excuse me

- Gomen nasai = I'm sorry

Navigating Common Situations

While those were some of the important phrases you might use as greetings or in a polite manner, also remember to equip yourself with some phrases that help you navigate some common situations like making small inquiries, asking common questions, or even ordering food for yourself. While many people tend to rely on online translation, that can be considered a risky option, considering the several complaints of the inaccuracy of these features. To avoid any kind of trouble here are a few phrases that might be helpful for you (Yoko,2020):

- O-tazune shite mo ii desu ka? = May I ask you a question?

- wa doko desu ka? = Where is ~?

- Chizu o kaite moraemasu ka? = Can you please draw a map for me?

- Koko wa doko desu ka? = Where am I?

- Chikaku ni o-susume no resutoran wa arimasu ka? = Are there any recommended restaurants nearby?

- Menu o kudasai = Please give me a menu

- Chumon o onegashimasu = I'm ready to order

- O-susume no menu wa dore desu ka? = What menu item do you recommend?

- Kore o onegaishimasu = I'd like (to order) this, please

Cultural Insights Through Language

An important thing to remember is that language isn't everything. For a place and people that value culture the way they do, you need to remember the cultural aspect that language represents for them. From your body language to small words of respect, the Japanese people notice everything. And you might find a few who can be a little quick to judge. Here are some things that you can remember that can make you more likable and respectful in their eyes:

Expressions Reflecting Politeness

Believe it or not, Japan considers the prospect of showing respect and politeness in high regard. You will find that not only do they have a few phrases used to address people

respectfully but they also have three whole types of honorific expressions that they use (Talkpal,2023).

- **Sonkeigo** is used for people who are at a higher level and need to be respected. This can include your boss, teacher or some elder. You might use different terminology compared to your normal terminology when talking to someone like that. For example: Taberu is a common word for eating but when used with sonkeigo it becomes meshiagaru.

- **Kenjougo** is used mostly in corporate settings and is also known as the humble language in which you show humility when addressing yourself. You can use it when making a request.

- **Teineigo**, also known as the polite language, is the most commonly used to be polite to people regardless of their social standing. This includes using words like 'sans 'which means Mr. or Ms. or 'masu or desu 'which are used after verbs to show respect.

Customs and Traditions in Daily Phrases

A place with such rich cultural heritage has some traditions set in place that they follow to this date and it would do good for you to remember those to fit in. It is more than just about learning a few sentences, but rather remembering a set of etiquettes they follow. Here is a list to help you (Maikoya, 2024):

- Bowing to show respect as a form of greeting.

- Avoiding physical touch.

- Removing your shoes before entering someone's house.

- Before starting to eat, wait for the host to say "itadakimasu" (I gratefully receive).

- Not speaking in loud volume in public.

- No tipping, people there can consider it offensive.

- Showering before using the onsen.

Cultural Nuances in Non-Verbal Communication

There are several things that hold a different meaning in Japan compared to other countries. It is important to know what kind of message you might be sending across to people in Japan using non-verbal communication and how different the meanings can be here. Let me give you some examples (Quezergue, 2023):

- The thumbs-down gesture there can be interpreted as a middle finger in Japan.

- PDA is often frowned upon except for holding hands.

- Avoiding eye contact can be considered as a sign of respect.

- Silence can also be a sign of respect in Japan.

Key Takeaways

- Try to avoid having a hard time by learning a few important phrases in Japanese.

- Remember that people in Japan value respect and politeness.

- Be mindful of your actions and gestures by remembering what they mean in Japanese culture.

100 Tips to Consider

1. Verify your country's visa requirements before traveling to Japan. Up to 70 countries have visa exemptions for traveling to Japan.
2. Book flights in advance for better deals.
3. Make sure your passport's validity extends 6 months beyond the end date of your travel duration.
4. Purchase travel insurance to cover any unforeseen circumstances. We recommend purchasing higher cover if engaging in sport activities like skiing/snowboarding
5. Carry emergency contact numbers with you.
6. Choose the best time to visit Japan based on weather and tourist seasons and preference of Japanese experience.
7. The plug type in Japan is "Type A"
8. Pack appropriate clothing for Japan's vast climate.
9. Don't forget to pack a swimsuit and towels for hot springs or beaches.
10. Gain insight into Japan's centuries-old sumo tradition by visiting a sumo stable to observe morning practice sessions. Witness the rigorous training regimen of sumo wrestlers, experience the intense atmosphere of the dohyo (sumo ring).
11. Always carry your passport on you; as a foreigner you are exempt on taxes on purchases and all you have to do is show it on check out.
12. Sample authentic Japanese cuisine like sushi, ramen, and tempura.
13. Rent a pocket Wi-Fi device or get a local SIM card for internet access.
14. Learn basic Japanese phrases to communicate with locals.
15. Use public transportation like trains and buses to get around efficiently.
16. Respect Japanese customs and etiquette, such as bowing and removing shoes indoors. Make sure to take off your shoes before entering homes, temples, certain traditional restaurants, and areas with tatami matting.
17. Wear comfortable shoes, some areas of Japan tourists wind up doing a lot of walking when exploring
18. Train etiquette, Japanese people do not take phone calls or eat while on the train. We suggest doing the same.

19. Taxi's are really expensive. Make taxis your last resort of mode of transport

20. Embrace the unique experiences Japan has to offer, from staying in a traditional ryokan to participating in a tea ceremony.

21. Visit Japan's iconic landmarks like Mount Fuji, Kyoto's temples, and Tokyo's bustling districts.

22. There are next to no public trash cans throughout Tokyo and the rest of Japan. Be prepared to carry your litter or keep a small bag to store it till you get back to your hotel.

23. Take advantage of Japan's efficient bullet trains to explore multiple cities.

24. Try seasonal activities like cherry blossom viewing in spring or skiing in winter.

25. Look into getting a "JR Pass" if your plan is to explore multiple cities, getting this in your home city is significantly cheaper than getting it in Japan. If you do this the pass will be sent directly to you.

26. 'IC card" or "Suica card"is a metro rail card that you can use to pay for the transport. You can tap your IC card when getting on and off the metro and you will get billed the required amount for the journey directly off the card.

27. You can use your Suica card for vending machine purchases at the stations.

28. Visit local izakayas (Japanese pubs) to experience casual dining and socializing.

29. Take time to relax and unwind in Japan's natural hot springs.

30. Great food can be found at convenience stores like Konbinis and 7Eleven.

31. Explore Japan's diverse landscapes, from scenic mountains to pristine beaches.

32. Visit historical sites like castles, temples, and shrines to learn about Japan's rich heritage.

33. Learn about Japan's history and culture by visiting museums and art galleries.

34. Take scenic hikes or nature walks in Japan's national parks and forests.

35. Use the application "Yelp" to find the best shops and restaurants.

36. It is legal to drink alcohol on the street in Japan.

37. Tipping is not needed in Japan.

38. Visit Japan's iconic landmarks at different times of the day to see them in different lights.
39. Carry cash (Japanese Yen) with you at all times, some places do not accept card.
40. The toilets in Japan are much different to those in the rest of the world. They have controls to the side of them which can be used to operate it. Familiarise yourself with it beforehand.
41. Enjoy the tranquility of Japanese gardens and parks, perfect for relaxation and reflection.
42. Take a leisurely stroll through historic neighborhoods and traditional villages.
43. Explore Japan's culinary scene by trying regional specialties and street food.
44. Experience the excitement of Japan's vibrant nightlife, from karaoke bars to izakayas.
45. Visit local markets and food stalls to sample fresh seafood and produce.
46. Try your hand at Japanese cooking by taking a cooking class or food tour.
47. Tap water is drinkable in Japan
48. Like Italy and other countries there is a charge to sit and eat in restaurants.
49. Water is free with all meals in restaurants.
50. Visit historical landmarks and cultural sites to learn about Japan's rich heritage.
51. Take scenic train journeys through Japan's picturesque countryside.
52. Explore Japan's natural beauty by hiking in national parks and exploring coastal areas.
53. Experience the tranquility of Japanese gardens and temples.
54. Discover hidden gems in Japan's lesser-known destinations.
55. Hotel rooms in Japan for the most part are small. Prepare for this
56. Plan a way from the airport if traveling to Tokyo as it is quite a distance from the city
57. The metros in Japan stop running around 11pm-1pm (at the latest) at night.
58. Visit historical sites and museums to learn about Japan's fascinating history.

59. Yamato is a luggage delivery service where if moving from one location to another with luggage you can organise Yamato to take your luggage for you to enjoy a handsfree transfer. Yamato does take a couple of days preplanning.

60. Narita Airport has luggage delivery services.

61. Make sure that your mobile device is equipped with Google Maps, Google Translate, and Hyperdia (an app to search train routes)

62. The Japanese experience is incomplete without sake tasting! You can go on a brewery tour or ask for recommendations from any bar or restaurant staff.

63. Explore Japan's diverse wildlife by visiting national parks and nature reserves.

64. Take a scenic boat ride on one of Japan's beautiful rivers or lakes.

65. Plan and time your sightseeing spots beforehand to avoid massive crowds.

66. Participate in a traditional Japanese calligraphy class to learn the art of brush writing.

67. Smoking indoors inside Japanese restaurants and bars is still very common.

68. Brush up on your chopstick etiquette. Never point them at someone, wave them in the air, or spear food with them.

69. Take a guided tour of Japan's bustling fish markets to see the variety of seafood on offer.

70. Experience the thrill of watching a baseball game, Japan's most popular sport.

71. Take your prescription with you if taking medication

72. Explore Japan's underground music scene by attending live concerts and performances.

73. Book restaurants and other activities in advance

74. Experience the Japanese Onsen for a luxurious and relaxing time. You can choose an indoor setting or an outdoor scenic view.

75. Visit a traditional ryokan (Japanese inn) for an authentic cultural experience.

76. Explore Japan's modern architecture and futuristic cityscapes in cities like Tokyo and Osaka.

77. Take a leisurely stroll through Japan's charming old towns and historic neighborhoods.

78. Visit the tropical beaches of Okinawa.

79. Go by the photography rules when you visit a museum or historical site.

80. Dress modestly when you visit such places. Cover yourself from your shoulders, all the way to your knees.

81. Carry a small bag with essentials, especially a towel and hand sanitizer. Some public bathrooms there don't have dryers, soap, or towels.

82. Make sure to inform your bank or credit/debit card providers about your travel so you can use your international card when needed without problems.

83. Alternatively using "WISE" bank, as they are international.

84. Dietary restrictions are not well understood in Japan so be precise and clear about allergies and anything you cannot eat at the time of ordering food.

85. Venture outside the cities especially if it's your first trip. Visit the islands, peaceful villages, and the wilderness of Hokkaido.

86. Research the opening hours and days of an attraction before making your way there.

87. Don't miss out on famous destination spots in Osaka such as Dotonbori. Try local delicacies such as octopus balls, grilled pancakes, and authentic Japanese BBQ.

88. Don't be afraid to use lockers at train stations and subways. This is the perfect way to store your luggage while you explore.

89. While walking and using escalators, most places stand on the left side. However, some places like Osaka, Wakayama and Nara stand on the right side. Be sure to observe the people in front of you.

90. Use activity booking apps like 'GetYourGuide' to book activities throughout the country, like go karting through the Toyko streets.

91. Attend the annual Sapporo Snow Festival held in the beginning of February, to see some of the most stellar ice sculptures.

92. Keep your cell phone on silent when visiting public places.

93. Don't blow your nose in public as it is considered highly rude.

94. It's will come as no surprise that taxi doors open automatically in Japan, Japan is known for its efficiency and advanced technologies.

95. Covering tattoos; There is still a perception in Japan that links tattoos to organized crime. As a foreigner you will likely not be mistaken. However, if you wish to utilize public spaces like gyms, swimming pools, and onsen, you might have to cover up your tattoos.

96. There are tattoo friendly onsens available

97. Maintain queues and wait in lines for your turn at any public place or attraction.

98. Avoid pointing fingers. Instead, try to use your hand or palm for gestures. Pointing is considered rude

99. Be sure to book hotels months in advance especially during Japan's busy seasons (first week of January) (late March-April) (April 25th-May 5th) and August

100. Research beforehand and see if it is cheaper for you to get to your accommodation in Tokyo via Haneda airport rather than Narita airport

References

Acar, A. (2020, November 2). *Kyoto's 5 Geisha Districts, History, Festivals, Main Differences in Traditions, Crests*. MAIKOYA. https://mai-ko.com/travel/culture-in-japan/geisha/kyotos-5-geisha-districts-history-festivals-main-differences-in-traditions-crests/

About Yokohama | Yokohama Official Visitors Guide - Travel Guide to Yokohama City. (n.d.). Yokohama. https://www.yokohamajapan.com/about/

Atherton, A. (2024). *Best Tea Houses in Kyoto for Japanese Tea Ceremony, Wagashi & More*. Byfood. https://www.byfood.com/blog/best-kyoto-tea-houses-p-516

Auras insurance. (n.d.). Travel insurance to Japan. Auras. https://auras.insure/travel-insurance-asia/japan/?utm_source=google&utm_medium=cpc&utm_campaign=k6&utm_content=ads2&utm_term=travel%20insurance%20for%20japan%20trip/&gad_source=1&gclid=CjwKCAjwzN-vBhAkEiwAYiO7oJm22Z_k9xi6y_ZBPjK3bVl29HSQcgUjZ6sK-65cAgideOAuras Insurance. (n.d.). *Travel insurance to Japan | Auras*. https://auras.insure/travel- insurance-asia/japan/?

Bernhard, F. (2024, February 9). *Tokyo: Exploring the Thriving Metropolis of Japan 2024*. Seikatsumi. https://seikatsumi.com/tokyo-exploring-the-thriving-metropolis-of-japan/

Brown, H. (n.d.). *10 Best Things to Do in Beppu - What is Beppu Most Famous For? - Go Guides*. Hotels.com Australia. https://au.hotels.com/go/japan/best-things-to-do- beppu

Brown, J. (2023, December 28). *Public Transportation in Japan: getting around in Japan*. EJable. https://www.ejable.com/japan-corner/travel-in-japan/transportation-in-japan/

Context Travel. (2023). *Your Guide to Tokyo's Food Scene - Context Travel. Your Guide to Tokyo's Food Scene - Context Travel*. https://www.contexttravel.com/blog/articles/tokyo-food-tours-guide

Chureito Pagoda. (n.d.). Fuji five lakes travel. https://www.japan-guide.com/e/e6917.html

Dayman, L. (2021, May 20). *Gion Kyoto: 20 Must-See Highlights of the Geisha District.*

Japan Objects. https://japanobjects.com/features/gion-kyoto

Dimitrijevic, U. (2019, August 14). *6 Ancient Japanese Traditions to Learn About Before Your Trip to Japan.* ACIS Educational Tours. https://acis.com/blog/ancient- traditions-you-might-see-on-your-student-tour-to-japan/

Dig-in to Japan's culinary paradise. (n.d.). JAL.https://www.jal.co.jp/sg/en/guide-to-japan/destinations/articles/osaka/dig-in-to-japan-culinary-paradise.html

8 Most Beautiful Lakes in Hokkaido. (n.d.). Kyuhoshi. https://www.kyuhoshi.com/lakes- in-hokkaido/

Flyer, G. (2023, January 27). *23 Best Iconic and Cultural Things to Do in Tokyo.*

Gourmetflyer.com. https://gourmetflyer.com/things-to-do-in-tokyo/

Food in Japan: 32 popular dishes you need to try on your next visit. (2023, June 15). LIVE JAPAN. https://livejapan.com/en/article-a0002670/

15 Awesome Things To Do In Beppu In 2024 | Travel Guide. (n.d.). Sugoii Japan. https://sugoii-japan.com/best-things-to-do-in-beppu

5 Must-Visit Nara Temples and Shrines: Discover the Timeless Beauty of Japan's Ancient Capital | LIVE JAPAN travel guide. (n.d.). LIVE JAPAN. https://livejapan.com/en/in-kansai/in-pref-nara/in- nara_ikoma_tenri/article-a2000164/

4 facts about the deer of Nara (n.d.). Nara travelers guide. https://narashikanko.or.jp/en/feature/deer/

Guide to Hiking Mount Rishiri (利尻山) in Japan. (n.d.). Halfway Anywhere. https://www.halfwayanywhere.com/trails/japan-hikes/hiking-mount-rishiri-rishizan-guide/

Gion - Kyoto Travel. (2022, July 19). Japan Guide. https://www.japan-guide.com/e/e3902.html

Google Arts & Culture. (n.d.). *9 World Heritage sites to explore in Okinawa - Google Arts & Culture*. https://artsandculture.google.com/story/9-world-heritage-sites-to- explore-in-okinawa-okinawa-prefecture/jgUxoSjGSDsGIg?hl=en

Hokkaido. (n.d.). GaijinPot Travel. https://travel.gaijinpot.com/destination/hokkaido/

Hokkaido's Best Parks and Nature Attractions - JAPAN AIRLINES. (n.d.). JAL. https://www.jal.co.jp/it/en/guide-to-japan/destinations/articles/hokkaido/best-parks-and-nature-attractions.html

Hells of Beppu | Travel Japan. (n.d.). Japan National Tourism Organization. https://www.japan.travel/en/spot/713/

Hot Springs Are Not Just For Bathing?! Four Other Ways To Enjoy Onsen - Enjoy Onsen. (2018, June 30). enjoy onsen japan hot spring beppu. https://enjoyonsen.city.beppu-jp.com/travel-tips/fourotherways_enjoyonsen/

Hotels. (2024). *24 Best Temples and Shrines in Kyoto - Kyoto's Most Important Shines and Temples - Go Guides*. Hotels.com. https://www.hotels.com/go/japan/best-kyoto-temples.

Hiroshima - Wikipedia. (n.d.). https://en.m.wikipedia.org/wiki/Hiroshima

In Japan's North, the Seasons Are Intense: 5 Gorgeous Places for Hokkaido Scenery | LIVE JAPAN travel guide. (2021, February 10). Live Japan. https://livejapan.com/en/in-hokkaido/in-pref-hokkaido/in-obihiro/article-a1000226/

ICAN. (2017). Hiroshima and Nagasaki bombings. https://www.icanw.org/hiroshima_and_nagasaki_bombings

Japan's diverse geography_ from mountains to coastlines.pdf - Japan, an archipelago in East Asia. (2023). Collegesidekick https://www.collegesidekick.com/study-docs/718585collegesidekick. (2023). Japan's Diverse Geography_ From Mountains to Coastlines. Collegesidekick. https://www.collegesidekick.com/study-docs/718585

Japan Experience. (2022). *Japan Geography*. Japan-Experience.com. https://www.japan-experience.com/plan-your-trip/to-know/traveling-japan/japan-geography

Japan Guide. (2023, August 21). *Japan's UNESCO World Heritage Sites*. Japan-Guide.com. https://www.japan-guide.com/e/e2251.html

Japan | History, Flag, Map, Population, & Facts. (2024, March 8). Britannica. https://www.britannica.com/place/Japan

Japan Rail Pass (JR Pass) - Trains. (2023, October 1). Japan Guide. https://www.japan-guide.com/e/e2361.html

Japan travel. (2024). *Cultural Experiences in Tokyo | Itineraries | Travel Japan - Japan National Tourism Organization (Official Site)*. Japan National Tourism Organization (JNTO). https://www.japan.travel/en/itineraries/hands-on-experiences-in-the-city/

Japan Rail Pass | Guide | Travel Japan. (n.d.). Japan National Tourism Organization. https://www.japan.travel/en/guide/jr-rail-pass/

Japan National Tourism Organization. (n.d.). *Top 10 unique flavours to explore in Japan*

- Japan National Tourism Organization. Japan National Tourism Organization (JNTO). https://www.japan.travel/en/au/story/top-10-unique-flavours-explore-japan

Japan, T. (n.d.). *Island Life: Okinawan culture and traditions*. Travel Japan. https://traveljapan.com.au/island-life-okinawan-culture-and-traditions

Japan Guide. (n.d.). *Lake Kawaguchiko. Fuji Five Lakes Travel*. https://www.japan-guide.com/e/e6906.html

Kyoto Travel. (2024). *About Kyoto | Kyoto City Official Travel Guide*. Kyoto City Official Travel Guide. https://kyoto.travel/en/about_kyoto.html

Live Japan. (2018). *10 Tokyo Cultural Experiences to Get to Know Japan First-Hand | LIVE JAPAN travel guide*. LIVE JAPAN. https://livejapan.com/en/article-a0001477/

Live Japan. (2020, April 26). *12 Unique Tokyo Neighborhoods & Districts You'll Want to Wander Around!* LIVE JAPAN. https://livejapan.com/en/article-a0002322/

Live Japan. (2023, April 13). *Best things to do in Gion: How to enjoy Kyoto's Geisha District*. LIVE JAPAN. https://livejapan.com/en/in-kansai/in-pref-kyoto/in-

gion_kawaramachi_kiyomizu-dera-temple/article-
a2000741/#:~:text=Here%2C%20you'll%20find%20charming,perfect%20for%2
0a%20relaxing%20stroll.

Live Japan. (2020, June 26). *Healthcare in Japan for tourists: What to do when you get sick or injured in Japan.* LIVE JAPAN. https://livejapan.com/en/article-a0002612/

MayaIncaAztec. (2019, November 3). *Ancient Japanese Customs.* MayaIncaAztec.com. https://www.mayaincaaztec.com/medievel-japan/ancient-japanese-customs

McElhinney, D. (n.d.). *Best time to visit Japan – Lonely Planet.* Lonely Planet.

https://www.lonelyplanet.com/articles/best-time-to-travel-to-japan

Maikoya. (2024, January 30). *Japanese culture and traditions.* Tea Ceremony Japan Experiences MAIKOYA. https://mai-ko.com/travel/culture-in-japan/japanese-culture-1/

Nara's Sacred Deer. (n.d.). https://www.visitnara.jp/venues/S01487/

Nara, V. (2016, September 11). *Traditional Crafts - Visit Nara.* https://www.visitnara.jp/lists-and-stories/story/amp/traditional-crafts/

Osaka: A Food Paradise. (2019, March 7). Eat the Wind. https://eatthewind.com/2019/03/07/osaka-a-food-paradise/

Osaka Castle | Discover Kansai. (n.d.). OSAKA-INFO. https://osaka-info.jp/en/discover-kansai/osaka-castle/

Osaka Food Markets: Everything You Need to Know. (2024, February 18). Trip To Japan. https://www.triptojapan.com/blog/osaka-food-markets-everything-you-need-to-know

Okinawa, Japan. (n.d.). Blue Zones. https://www.bluezones.com/explorations/okinawa-japan/

Osaka Nightlife & Party Guide – 2024. (2024, January 10). Nightlife Party Guide. https://nightlifepartyguide.com/osaka-nightlife-party-guide/

Official Okinawa Travel Guide. (2024, February 20). *Beaches of Central and Southern Okinawa - VISIT OKINAWA JAPAN | Official Okinawa Travel Guide.* VISIT

OKINAWA JAPAN | Official Okinawa Travel Guide.
https://visitokinawajapan.com/discover/beach-information/beaches-central-southern-okinawa/

Official Okinawa Travel Guide. (2024b, February 20). *Okinawa's Traditional Calendar - VISIT OKINAWA JAPAN | Official Okinawa Travel Guide.* VISIT OKINAWA JAPAN | Official Okinawa Travel Guide. https://visitokinawajapan.com/discover/traditional-culture/okinawa-traditional-calendar/

Owen, A. (2019, September 10). *Japan Travel Tips: Expert Advice for an Amazing Trip.*

Boutique Japan. https://boutiquejapan.com/japan-travel-tips/

Port, A. (2023, October 4). *When Is the Best Time to Visit Japan?* Conde Nast Traveler. https://www.cntraveler.com/story/best-time-to-visit-japan

P. Rafferty, J. (2024, February 16). *Volcanism | Examples, Effects, & Facts.* Encyclopedia Britannica. https://www.britannica.com/science/volcanism

Promoting Initiatives for the Abolition of Nuclear Weapons - 広島市公式ホームページ

| 国際平和文化都市. (n.d.).

https://www.city.hiroshima.lg.jp/site/english/247321.html

Quezergue, C. (2023, May 2). 15 Unique Facts about Japanese Communication | CoTo Academy. Coto Academy. https://cotoacademy.com/unique-facts-about-japanese-communication/#:~:text=What%20are%20some%20common%20nonverbal,can

%20convey%20friendliness%20and%20warmth.

Rowthorn, W. B. C. (2024, February 8). *Kyoto Ryokan - Inside Kyoto.* Inside Kyoto. https://www.insidekyoto.com/kyoto-ryokan

Rakuten Travel. (n.d.). *A guide to Tokyo's best capsule hotels.*

https://travel.rakuten.com/contents/usa/en-us/best-capsule-hotels-tokyo

Simple guide to money when travelling in Japan. (2019, September 8). Traveling Honeybird. https://www.travelinghoneybird.com/money-guide-travellin-japan/

S.V. (2020). *Japan, the land of the rising sun: meaning and origin.* Japan-
    Experience.com. https://www.japan-experience.com/plan-your-trip/to-
    know/understanding-japan/japan-land-of-the-rising-sun-meaning

studyinjpn. (2023). *What kind of country is Japan? Introducing basic information and
    features of Japan in various languages ｜ Guide to study in Japan | 日本留学ナビ*
    . Studyinjpn.com. https://studyinjpn.com/column/about_japan

So You've Landed In Japan – Arrival Procedures. (2020, February 25). Jose's Japan Tips.
    https://myjapantips.com/2020/02/25/so-youve-landed-in-japan-arrival-
    procedures/

Sapporo Snow Festival. (n.d.). Travel Japan. https://www.japan.travel/en/spot/473/

Shinjuku: The Heart of Tokyo's Nightlife and Entertainment. (2024, March 10). Trip To
    Japan. https://www.triptojapan.com/blog/shinjuku-the-heart-of-tokyo-s-
    nightlife-and-entertainment

Shinkansen: Bullet Trains in Japan | JRailPass. (n.d.). Japan Rail Pass.
    https://www.jrailpass.com/shinkansen-bullet-trains

Sasaki, D. (2024, February 4). *Hakone: 5 Budget-Friendly luxurious Ryokans with
    private onsen - The Luxury Japan.* The Luxury Japan.
    https://theluxuryjapan.com/top-5-hakone-ryokan-luxury-recommendations-
    from-locals/

Sasaki, D. (2024b, February 24). *11 Most expensive and luxurious hotels in Tokyo 2024
    - The Luxury Japan.* The Luxury Japan. https://theluxuryjapan.com/most-
    expensive-luxurious-hotels-in-tokyo/

*Story of cities #24: how Hiroshima rose from the ashes of nuclear destruction | Cities |
    The Guardian.* (n.d.). https://amp.theguardian.com/cities/2016/apr/18/story-of-
    cities-hiroshima-japan-nuclear-destruction

Travel, K. (n.d.). Your guide to Japan's epic autumn festivals. Klook
    https://www.klook.com/blog/japans-epic-autumn-festivals/

Tea, S. (2019, September 4). *Unveiling Kyoto's Finest Tea Houses: A Journey Through
    Tradition - Senbird Tea.* Senbird Tea. https://senbirdtea.com/blogs/travel/3-
    traditional-japanese-tea-houses-to-visit-in-kyoto

10 Reasons Why Osaka is a Street Food Lovers Paradise. (2020, September 7). YouFoundSarah. https://youfoundsarah.com/osaka-strect-food/

T, G. N. (2022, June 13). Asahidake, Japan: The mountain where Ainu gods play. SPACE STORIES by GIFT.

https://spacestoriesbygift.wordpress.com/2022/06/13/asahidake-ropeway-daisetsuzan/

Tham, E. (2024, March 11). *Where to Ski in Hokkaido: 7 Best Ski Resorts in Hokkaido to Check Out.* Klook. https://www.klook.com/en-SG/blog/best-ski-resorts-in-hokkaido/

Tokyo Nightlife: Shibuya vs. Roppongi - Trip To Japan. (2024, March 10). Trip To Japan. https://www.triptojapan.com/blog/tokyo-nightlife-shibuya-vs-roppongi

The Rarest Onsen in Japan?! The "Sunayu" Feature Article - Enjoy Onsen. (2018, March 26). enjoy onsen japan hot spring beppu. https://enjoyonsen.city.beppu-jp.com/travel-tips/sunayu/

Tan, B. (2023, October 24). *Trains in Japan: First-Timer's Guide to Japan's Rail Network.* Klook. https://www.klook.com/blog/trains-in-japan-guide/

Train Travel in Japan: A Comprehensive Guide. (n.d.). Boutique Japan. https://boutiquejapan.com/train-travel-in-japan/

Traditional Crafts of Nara. (2020, January 19). https://nara-sightseeing.com/blog/nara-traditional-crafts-part1/

TalkPal. (2023, June 8). *Honorific Expressions in Japanese Grammar - TalkPal.*

https://talkpal.ai/grammar/honorific-expressions-in-japanese-grammar/

Voyapon. (2020, August 24). *VOYAPON - Discover the Rich Heritage of Japanese Culture.* VOYAPON. https://voyapon.com/interests/culture/

van Hout, N. (2023, March 16). *10 Essential Travel Apps For Japan.* The Navigatio. https://thenavigatio.com/travel-apps-for-japan/

VisitLaos.org. (2024, March 21). *Embark on a gastronomic adventure in Japan's culinary capital.* Visit Laos – Untouched Nature.

https://www.visitlaos.org/global-travel-news/embark-on-a-gastronomic-adventure-in-japans-culinary-capital/

Wada, Y. (2023, August 16). *Tokyo Food Guide 2023: Top 5 Foods You Need to Try.* Ninja Food Tours. https://www.ninjafoodtours.com/tokyo-food-guide/

What is onsen(Hot spring)? (n.d.). 日本温泉協会. https://www.spa.or.jp/en/onsen/

War Memorials. (n.d.). https://www.japan-guide.com/e/e7105.html

Web Japan. (n.d.). *Initiatives for Public Hygiene in Japan | Web Japan.* https://web-japan.org/trends/11_tech-life/tec202008_wash-hands.html#:~:text=They%20wash%20their%20hands%20and,customs%20for%20people%20in%20Japan.

Web Japan. (n.d.-a). *Disaster Education in Japan: Preparing for natural disasters to protect kids 'lives | Web Japan.* https://web-japan.org/kidsweb/cool/20/202011_disaster-prevention-education_en.html

World heritage. (n.d.). https://dive-hiroshima.com/en/feature/world-heritage/

Xie, A. C. a. Q. (2024, March 21). *Cherry blossom season in Japan: where and when to go in 2024. The Times.* https://www.thetimes.co.uk/travel/destinations/asia-travel/japan/guide-to-cherry-blossom-holidays-in-japan-tjl2v0q3p#:~:text=The%20earliest%20blooms%20tend%20to,April%20is%20a%20good%20bet.

Yoko. (2020, September 29). *Japanese are so polite! 52 Weirdly useful phrases to understand Japanese manners & daily life.* LIVE JAPAN. https://livejapan.com/en/in-tokyo/in-pref-tokyo/in-tokyo_train_station/article-a0003255/

Zipper, D. (2022, September 7). Bloomberg. https://www.bloomberg.com/news/articles/2022-09-06/what-drove-japan-s-remarkable-traffic-safety-turnaround

Zerkalenkov, Z. (2022, December 2). *Wellness Tourism in Japan: The Ultimate Guide.* Travel Content Creators. https://www.travelcontentcreators.com/wellness-tourism-japan/

Made in United States
Cleveland, OH
04 March 2025

14810157R00079